Raising Emotionally Intelligent Children:

Introduction to Emotional Intelligence

Dr. B. L. Buddy Fish

Gifts

We are given gifts –
Control, Ambition, and Freedom.
All of them are good.
None of them are bad.

We receive the need to control, but
Taken to extremes
Could lead to
Fear of change
Suppression of new ideas, or
Intolerance of anything different.

We receive the gift of ambition or motivation, but
Taken to extremes
Leads to the determination to seize power at all costs,
Enslavement.
Desires can become obsessions
Leading to greed, lust, avarice, and
Jealousy.

We receive the gift of freedom, but
Taken to extremes is
Anarchy.

We learn moderation.

Anonymous

Library of Congress Cataloging-in-Publication Data

Fish, Barney L.

    Raising Emotionally Intelligent Children: Introduction to Emotional Intelligence/Barney L. Buddy Fish

    p. cm.

    Includes bibliographic references.

    ISBN 978-0-578-07644-7

    1. Emotional intelligence.   2. Interpersonal skills for families.   3. Families   4. Early Childhood Education
I. Fish, Barney L.   II. Title

©AMF Books: A part of FISHYRHYTHMSPUBLISHING, LLC

200 E. Capitol Street
Ste. 1600
Jackson, MS 39201

Copyright Applied for © 2011 by AMF Books, Ridgeland, Mississippi 39157. All rights reserved. Printed in the United States of America. This publication is protected by Copyright and permission should be obtained from the publisher prior to any prohibited reproduction, storage in a retrieval system, or transmission in any form or by any means, electronic, mechanical, photocopying, recording, or likewise. For information regarding permission(s), write to: Rights and Permissions Department.

ISBN 978-0-578-07644-7

Table of Contents

Part I

    Introduction..1

    Chapter 1..2
        Protecting our Future
    Chapter 2..15
        The Role of the Early Childhood Educator
    Chapter 3..32
        Changing Brain Physiology Though Affective Education
    Chapter 4..39
        Emotional Intelligence with Families and Educators

Part II 46
    Practical Ways to Teach and Think About Emotional Intelligence

References..82

Appendix A   Feelings Words

Introduction

In an era when children frequently feel disconnected from friends and family, where rapid social change is the norm, when media and sports stars demonstrate poor behavior, educators recognize the human need for developing social and emotional skills. At the same time, school budgets are being cut while pressure is being intensified to improve test scores – leaving many educators with a perceived dichotomy. They believe the choice is either nurture children or help them achieve. Fortunately, the compelling evidence shows that it is not an either/or choice; rather, the data says addressing children's social and emotional needs is an effective way to improve academic achievement.

Research has illustrated how EQ can substantially decrease anti-social behavior and aggression, school suspensions, and discipline problems while increasing personal and social competency, school attendance and completion, satisfaction, and academic achievement. (Cherniss, Extein, Goleman, Weissberg , 2006). This overwhelming body of new findings has led to a powerful conclusion that direct intervention in the psychological determinants of learning promise the most effective avenues of reform. Social and emotional development is central to children's success in school. By incorporating EQ into existing educational programs, we can promote our children's achievement in the present and secure their success for the future. Through our children's success, our country will excel in the global economy.

Chapter 1

Protecting our Future

We know that we need to prepare our children to participate in our society to successfully compete with the global economy, but what does the future hold for us? If we do not design our own future, someone else will design it for us. Our children need access to the creative enterprises that nourish the skills and sensitivities necessary to be ready to design a better future – self-knowledge with art, words and music to communicate their thoughts and feelings. For many years, we have placed great emphasis on teaching our children reading, science, and mathematics skills. Society has been more concerned with cognitive skills than emotional intelligence. While Western culture has recognized that emotions are important, less emphasis has been placed on understanding emotional than cognitive or physical development (Jensen, 1998). Marquis (1996) noted that psychology has been too atomized in the sense that it divided intelligence, motor skills, and emotions into different areas, rather than considering the inseparable links among them. These domains are interrelated and interdependent – growth in each depends upon and actuates growth in the others.

Ever since the publication of Goleman's first book on the topic in 1995, emotional intelligence has become one of the hottest buzzwords in corporate America. For instance, when the Harvard Business Review published an article on the topic, it attracted a higher percentage of readers than any other article published in that periodical in the last 40 years. When the CEO of Johnson & Johnson read that article, he was so impressed that he had copies sent out to the 400 top executives in the company worldwide.

Creativity and innovation come with exposure, practice and personal growth. To ignore the cultivation of these skill sets and aptitudes in an entire generation of children is a prescription for failure. If we want our children to be ready to compete in the global economy, we cannot continue to ignore this important domain of development. In this treatise, I will cite the research linking emotional intelligence with important outcomes such as individual performance and cognitive growth.

When does emotional intelligence begin to develop?

A child's emotional education begins before birth with the most rapid brain development occurring during the prenatal months. A stressful pregnancy can create future cognitive, motor, and emotional problems while planned parenthood can pre-establish an empathetic attitude for the child. Non-stressful birthing techniques offer opportunities to reduce tension from the beginning of life outside the womb (Jensen, 1998). Caregivers note that infants display emotional behavior prior to language development.

During the first 36 months of life, the brain is wiring itself to communicate with the rest of the body. Ledoux (1996) stated that it is not only the brain that affects cognitive and emotional growth, but also the communication between the brain and the rest of the body. It was formerly assumed that synapse was the only chemical that made animals react; today, medical professionals recognize that other chemicals involved in synapse such as seratonin, dopamine, and cortisol communicate with other parts of the body via peptides. Jensen (1998) refers to these peptides as the body's "emotional highway" (p. 75).

Goleman (1995) suggested that emotional balance has a greater bearing on success in today's world than does the Intelligence Quotient. Jensen (1998) cited that an analysis of emotional balance in reference to fetal and infant brain chemistry indicated that: "...[between] 0 and 18 months ... [infants need]... loving care, laughter, smiles...[parents should] bond with [the] child to avoid threats" (p. 86). Caregivers have classified infant emotional behavior prior to six months of age or [before] language development. Babies are described as bossy, temperamental, good natured, or easy to get along with. Izard & Read (1986) developed an emotional measurement scale used by many scientists to identify the affective states of infants and toddlers. This scale has been used to rate both the central nervous system and the autonomic nervous system responses to various stimuli in infants. Test results using these scales have validated the work of Piaget and Erikson.

Erikson's (1959) described conflict resolution or crisis dichotomy behaviors in terms of "oral reassurance" (p. 65). The initial balance between basic trust vs. basic mistrust does not seem to be related to the amount of food or demonstrations of love from the caregiver but to the quality of the parental relationship. The successful balance of trust is thought to translate into adults who are "...less dependent on mild or malignant forms of addiction, on self delusion, and on avaricious appropriation" (p. 64).

Ramey and Ramey (1999) maintain that infants cannot be given too much attention. Often well-meaning intelligent parents, who believe that their child should never have to cry to get to have needs met, misinterpret this trust issue. Similarly, these same informed parents want to force feed knowledge into their children at a young age because the brain is wiring itself so rapidly. Neither of these concepts are accurate. Research has shown that challenge creates growth; an infant's cry is its way of communicating needs. Secondly, putting this same infant in an inappropriate learning situation causes stress, which hinders emotional development (Jensen, 1998).

Infants, described by caregivers as bossy, temperamental, good- natured, or easy to get along with, display emotional development by six months of age (Coles, 1997). Erikson's (1959) conflict resolution or crisis dichotomy describes infant behaviors in terms of oral reassurance. The initial balance between basic trust versus basic mistrust is not related to the amount of food or demonstrations of love given to the infant but to the consistent quality of the bond between the infant and the caregiver relationship. The successful balance of trust is thought to translate into adults who were "...less dependent on mild or malignant forms of addiction, on self-delusion, and on avaricious appropriation" (Erikson, 1959, p. 64).

Caregivers, who believe that young children should never feel stressful or who provide excessive stimulation, also miss the differences between challenge and stress. Current research revealed that challenge creates growth; the infant who cries to have its needs met is learning to communicate.

What is Emotional Intelligence and how is it taught?

Young children develop emotional skills through interaction with family members and other children. Through social interactions they learn self-control, as well as sharing, playing together, and resolving problems. Young children learn these skills at home, during childcare, or within school environments that foster the development of positive emotional development. Young children develop emotional intelligence by seeing others model, through discussion, and from encouragement that help them learn to use positive rather than negative behaviors (Wortham, 2002).

The transition into school and the new roles to be encountered are of considerable importance in children from five to eight years of age. Aside from the issues of attachment, young children must make great emotional strides upon entrance to their new school environment. When young children first enter learning environments, caregivers must help them understand what behaviors are appropriate for school. Most children have learned the acceptable way to behave at home and believe this is the way they should operate in other environments. Some behaviors that are acceptable at home may not be appropriate at school. In the home environment children may be allowed to have confrontations with their siblings, but at school they must interact with their peers in a non-aggressive manner that avoids the use of force. Independence, assertiveness, sensitivity to others, and the willingness to participate in social problem solving have been identified as necessary traits for children to experience successful social experiences (Frost, Worthman, & Reifel, 2001). One technique for helping children develop emotional intelligence is through affective education.

Knowledge that emphasizes internal worlds in relationship to individuals is called affective education. This type of learning appears in various forms, such as encounter groups, sensitivity training programs, and executive management groups. These groups, made up largely of adults voluntarily seeking self-knowledge, share the belief that learning about one's self is an important and neglected part of the educational system and that shared experiences in a group setting facilitate such learning (Stone & Dillehunt, 1978). There are few forms of affective education designed for children.

Lev Vygotsky, a social psychologist, emphasized that children can learn from each other and adults through interactive experience. Bodrova and Leong (2007) used his theories to develop early childhood programs centered around play. Through play, children learn self regulation skills which are key elements in the emotional intelligence paradigm.

Some teachers adapt techniques of affective education; others experiment with the teaching of values or values clarification. The majority of affective education takes place in remediation courses as a means of teaching children when traditional techniques have failed in the form of effective character education. An effective character education program combines the teaching of specific skills with learning opportunities to clarify personal or group values by helping children learn about consequences and choices. A quality program enhances other kinds of learning and community appreciation. Character programs run the gamut from mechanisms to specific behaviors to vague plans, while other programs advocate elaborate systems of rewards and punishments. Emotional intelligence is the cornerstone of an acceptable character education program (Freedman, 2001). Some programs blend cognitive and affective education into a confluent education that emphasizes both cognitive and affective elements in any learning situation. The emotional intelligence curriculum is one such a program (McCown, Jensen, Freeman, & Rideout, 1998).

There are basic constructs that have been shown to characterize an emotionally intelligent person (Fish, 2008, Freeman, 2007). They can be grouped into three basic elements – self-knowledge, self-acceptance, and empathetic goal selection. We can further break these elements down into eight skills:

1. Emotional literacy – perceiving, understanding words to express emotion.
2. Patterns of behavior – comprehending how emotion affects our actions.
3. Consequential thinking – realizing costs and benefits of our actions and shifting adverse patterns.
4. Navigating emotions – changing and working with our emotions and delaying gratification.
5. Engaging intrinsic motivation – building internal devices toward perseverance.
6. Shifting to optimism – self efficacy to realize our own power and responsibility.
7. Empathy – expanding our feelings beyond ourselves.
8. Acting on our goals – begin to determine what we want from life.

In Part II we will further delve into these eight constructs of emotional intelligence (EQ). We will begin by introducing general principles and discoveries about the topic. We will then suggest some specific techniques for teaching EQ. An emotional intelligence curriculum is an experiential program designed for children in the primary grades to equip them with affective and cognitive skills to broaden their understanding and functioning in all learning and social situations. Students are taught to use scientific inquiry methods to study their inner selves. Students are taken from where they are emotionally to a point that they can look at themselves to help them discover their best learning styles and study habits. Through the process they are helped to rid themselves of emotional encumbrances which would ordinarily stand in their way toward academic and social success. Students are given opportunities to apply their emotional intelligence skills through frequent experiential assignments and periodic evaluation mechanisms (Stone & Dillehunt, 1978, 1998).

To summarize, the composition of the American family is changing, and the ability of parents to meet the affective needs of children is decreasing rapidly (Hernandez, 1995). Unfortunately, many parents lack emotional intelligence and cannot teach behaviors that they themselves lack to their children (Fish, 2008). Young children need to be taught emotional intelligence skills in a consistent, repetitive way that makes positive behaviors as automatic as negative ones. A goal of educators should be to help children develop emotional intelligence. Parents and Early Childhood Educators should take the responsibility for teaching these skills which are necessary for a good, healthy life (Goleman, 1997).

Historical Overview of Emotional Intelligence

When psychologists began to write and think about intelligence, they focused on cognitive aspects, such as memory and problem-solving. However, there were researchers who recognized early on that the non-cognitive aspects were also important. For instance, David Wechsler defined intelligence as "the aggregate or global capacity of the individual to act purposefully, to think rationally, and to deal effectively with his environment" (Wechsler, 1958, p. 7). As early as 1940 he referred to "non-intellective" as well as "intellective" elements (Wechsler, 1940), by which he meant affective, personal, and social factors. Furthermore, as early as 1943 Wechsler was proposing that the non-intellective abilities are essential for predicting one's ability to succeed in life. He wrote:

> The main question is whether non-intellective, that is affective and conative abilities, are admissible as factors of general intelligence. (My contention) has been that such factors are not only admissible but necessary. I have tried to show that in addition to intellective there are also definite non-intellective factors that determine

intelligent behavior. If the foregoing observations are correct, it follows that we cannot expect to measure total intelligence until our tests also include some measures of the non-intellective factors [Wechsler, 1943 #316, p. 103).

Wechsler was not the only researcher who saw non-cognitive aspects of intelligence to be important for adaptation and success. Robert Thorndike, to take another example, was writing about "social intelligence" in the late thirties (Thorndike & Stein, 1937). Unfortunately, the work of these early pioneers was largely forgotten or overlooked until 1983 when Howard Gardner began to write about "multiple intelligence." Gardner (1983) proposed that "intrapersonal" and "interpersonal" intelligences are as important as the type of intelligence typically measured by IQ and related tests.

IQ by itself is not a very good predictor of job performance. Hunter and Hunter (1984) estimated that at best IQ accounts for about 25 percent of the variance. Sternberg (1996) has pointed out that studies vary and that 10 percent may be a more realistic estimate. In some studies, IQ accounts for as little as 4 percent of the variance. An example of this research on the limits of IQ as a predictor is the Sommerville study, a 40 year longitudinal investigation of 450 boys who grew up in Sommerville, Massachusetts. Two-thirds of the boys were from welfare families, and one-third had IQ's below 90. However, IQ had little relation to how well they did at work or in the rest of their lives. What made the biggest difference was childhood abilities such as being able to handle frustration, control emotions, and get along with other people (Snarey & Vaillant, 1985).

Another good example is a study of 80 Ph.D.'s in science who underwent a battery of personality tests, IQ tests, and interviews in the 1950s when they were graduate students at Berkeley. Forty years later, when they were in their early seventies, they were tracked down and estimates were made of their success based on resumes, evaluations by experts in their own fields, and sources like American Men and Women of Science. It turned out that social and emotional abilities were four times more important than IQ in determining professional success and prestige (Feist & Barron, 1996).

It would be absurd to suggest that cognitive ability is irrelevant for success in science. One needs a relatively high level of such ability merely to get admitted to a graduate science program at a school like Berkeley. Once you are admitted, however, what matters in terms of how you do compared to your peers has less to do with IQ differences and more to do with social and emotional factors. To put it another way, if you're a scientist, you probably needed an IQ of 120 or so simply to get a doctorate and a job. But then it is more important to be able to persist in the face of difficulty and to get along well with colleagues and subordinates than it is to have an extra 10 or 15 points of IQ. The same is true in many other occupations.

We also should keep in mind that cognitive and non-cognitive abilities are very much related. In fact, there is research suggesting that emotional and social skills actually help improve cognitive functioning. For instance, in the famous "marshmallow studies" at Stanford University, four year olds were asked to stay in a room alone with a marshmallow and wait for a researcher to return. They were told that if they could wait until the researcher came back before eating the marshmallow, they could have two. Ten years later the researchers tracked down the kids who participated in the study. They found that the kids who were able to resist temptation had a total SAT score that was 210 points higher than those kids who were unable to wait (Shoda, Mischel, & Peake, 1990).

Granted that cognitive ability seems to play a rather limited role in accounting for why some people are more successful than others, what is the evidence that emotional and social factors are important? In doing the research for his first book, Goleman (1995) became familiar with a wealth of research pointing to the importance of social and emotional abilities for personal success. Some of this research came from personality and social psychology, and some came from the burgeoning field of neuropsychology. Let me give you an example that deals specifically with the role that non-cognitive abilities play in success at work and school.

Now let us switch our historical lens to psychology. In the 1940s, under the direction of Hemphill (1959), the Ohio State Leadership Studies suggested that "consideration" is an important aspect of effective leadership. More specifically, this research suggested that leaders who are able to establish mutual trust, respect, and a certain warmth and rapport with members of their group will be more effective (Fleishman & Harris, 1962). At about the same time, the Office of Strategic Services (1948) developed a process of assessment based on the earlier work of Murray (1938) that included the evaluation of non-cognitive, as well as cognitive, abilities. This process evolved into the "assessment center," which was first used in the private sector at AT&T in 1956 (Bray, 1976). Many of the dimensions measured in assessment centers then and now involve social and emotional competencies such as communication, sensitivity, initiative, and interpersonal skills (Thornton & Byham, 1982). It is not uncommon today for a person's intelligence to be evaluated and assigned a numerical rating due to performance on one standardized assessment. Such pencil-and-paper tests measure linguistic and mathematical proficiency. The concept of standardized tests began in the early 1900's with the works of Alfred Binet, a psychologist, who believed intelligence to be fixed and determined by genetics. Binet's commission from the French Minister of Education was to develop an instrument in order to measure then classify the intellectual inadequacies, rather than potentials, of an individual. The Intelligence Quotient, or IQ test as it became known, was to be utilized in identifying the incapacities of children to determine needed special educational assistance (Rosenthal & Jacobson, 1966). Labeling children according to their scores on single pencil-and-paper assessments became like a brand for each child to wear throughout the educational process. This practice often limited students' choices of academic courses and destroyed their chances for a higher education. As noted by Lohman (2003):

> The use of <u>intelligence</u> tests in the American education system is widespread despite the well documented {sic} shortcomings of these instruments. For instance, the fact that minority groups are overrepresented [sic] in special education and underrepresented {sic} in gifted and talented programs is but one example of how intelligence test scores, coupled with the results from other diagnostic instruments, are used daily to make decisions about eligibility for special programs. (p. 276)

While the term emotional intelligence is relatively new, the principles are founded in a long tradition. Plato wrote that all learning has an emotional base. The history of emotional education is imbedded into the history of early childhood education itself. In 1816, Robert Owen set up a nursery school in Great Britain to counteract bad influences of the home. Freidrich Froebel created the kindergarten as a place where children could flower. Sigmund Freud emphasized the value of a healthy emotional environment during childhood in 1905. Arnold Gessell began to study the importance of the preschool years in 1911. Rogers' client-centered methods (1969) in the field of clinical psychology stressed the importance of feelings and focusing on the learner rather than the teacher or the material to be taught. The field of early childhood education has always been predominantly child centered. The competent early childhood educator is much more interested in the total needs of the child rather that only academic needs (Morrison, 2001).

The modern movement to recognize the importance of the development of emotional intelligence has its roots in the self-actualization and motivational studies of Maslow (1943, 1969). Maslow's work inspired many students to look at more than cognitive-logical, information oriented educational techniques. It was proposed that basic needs are arranged in a hierarchy in which each level of need has to be met before successive levels of need can be addressed. Maslow's list of human needs (freedom from discomfort, physical safety, a sense of belonging, self-esteem, and intellectual growth) formed the basis for affective educators (Maslow, 1969; McCown, 1979).

Piaget (1962) recognized the interdependence of the affective and cognitive domains and theorized that there is no such thing as a purely cognitive state:

> There are no acts of intelligence, even of practical intelligence, without interest at the point of departure and affective regulation during the entire course of an action, without joy at success or sorrow at failure (p. 130).

Similarly, there can be no purely affective state. Even the simplest forms of affect presuppose some discrimination and hence a cognitive element. Cognition and affectivity are non-dissociable (p. 131).

The concept of confluent education proposed that affective, cognitive, and behavioral development occur together. It influenced the first emotional intelligence curriculum, Self-Science. Gestalt therapy became widely known for studying the individual in the context of the environment. These two factors led to teaching the whole child in its environment and became a mainstay for the constructivist movement (Steinberg, 1998). Model programs were developed to further examine the needs of the total child.

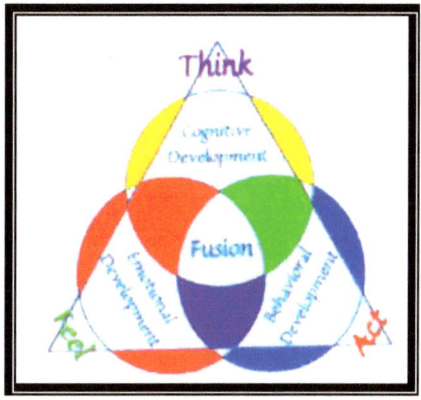

The Confluent Model

The Perry Project used the "Plan-Do-Review" program to encourage children to make choices about what they wanted to learn and how to accomplishment the learning. Learning experiences were selected from a list of key elements developed by the program creators. Individual learning was encouraged during work time; children functioned as a group only during the planning and review times. The Perry Project was a forerunner to the learning center approach to education (Schweinhart & Weikart, 1993). The seventies also brought the onset of humanistic-affective education programs. The University of Massachusetts School of Education presented a program where initial methods for self-concept development, values clarification, and conflict resolution were developed. This new methodology incorporated an emphasis on the process of education rather than the product. Educators began to realize that children learned through experience rather than recitation and regurgitation Some educators were opposed to humanistic-affective education because of the lack of methods to measure progress (McCown, 1978).

The educational community, wanting more qualitative measures in education, explored ethnographic research as a possible solution. The NAEYC proposed anecdotal methods to record children's progress (Caine & Caine,1994, 1997, Bredekamp & Copple, 1997, 2009). This solution provided educators with an opportunity to give credence to the larger human experience through narrative record keeping rather than simple numbers of right and wrong answers.

The direct teaching model was developed to insure that all students met a certain standardized norm of intelligence. Educators recognized the need for a new model or paradigm based on the concept that each individual is unique with different needs and strategies for learning. The constructivist approach to education evolved from Piagetian philosophy with a unique concept of learning. Instead of learners adjusting to the teacher, teachers recognize that each child is unique coming from different backgrounds, so each child learns differently. If a child does not learn, the weakness could be a teaching problem instead of a child problem. The movement toward giving more time and effort to developing not just cognitive skills, but also, affective skills in the classroom is continuing to spread in the field of education. The emotionally safe classroom is logically a classroom where more learning can take place (Bluestein, 2001).

Hoy (2001) suggested that a strong correlation existed between the learner's well being and the atmosphere in the educational environment. Educational theorists noted that a nonjudgmental, noncompetitive, cooperative and intimate teaching approach should exist at all times, not just during art hour. The learning environment must be emotionally safe with time available for helping children learn to respond to their emotions in acceptable ways. Students need practice to develop the necessary communication skills to express their thoughts and feeling in a socially acceptable manner. Teachers should serve as positive role models by sharing and expressing their feeling with the children and developing the power that comes from understanding the emotions felt by children (Russ, 2001).

Grinder and Bandler's models for more clearly recognizing individual learning styles and strategies and Dunn and Dunn's work with individual learning styles have become widely known and accepted as having merit (Steinberg, 1998). Gardner's theory of multiple intelligence indicated that all learners are capable of mastering skills in their individual ways. When educators empower learners by allowing them to discover their areas of intelligence, learners use their learning styles to master cognitive skills. Through becoming aware of their strengths and weaknesses, children develop self-awareness, a key element in emotional intelligence (McCown, 1998).

Naess (2000) proposed that during the school years the shaping and influencing of future adults takes place; "the seed is sowed that will determine how well we will fit into society" (p. 167). In a group of twenty kindergarten children, there will be at least one each of the main personalities or intelligences. Naess concluded with:

> It is only now that I realize what I could have done. I
> could have divided the children into different groups. I

could have organized the groups so that each group
included one of each [intelligence], so that there would
be seven different views and behaviors to relate to. I
would have understood why the children behaved and
acted so differently. I could have taught them teamwork.
They could have begun to understand how they depend
on each other, and how cooperation creates a
functioning team. I could have taught them that one
alone is nothing. Everybody is equally important, and
when they help each other to stay balanced positively that
they really help themselves. This would result in a feeling
of self-worth--the feeling that you are somebody, and that
the energies and talents you naturally bring to the world
are worth something. (pp.167-168)

Erickson (1959) reported that children develop their identity around age two and their sense of industriousness or self worth around age six. Twerski (2000) agreed that self-worth develops early in life; psychologically healthy people want the approval of others because they desire others to recognize their value. Psychologically unhealthy persons need approval from others to create their value "much like a light bulb which lights up only if the electric current flows" (p. 247).

Martin Seligman has developed a construct that he calls "learned optimism" (Schulman, 1995). It refers, among other things, to the causal attributions people make when confronted with failure or setbacks. Optimists tend to make specific, temporary, external causal attributions while pessimists make global, permanent, internal attributions. In research at Met Life, Seligman and his colleagues found that new salesmen who were optimists sold 37 percent more insurance in their first two years than did pessimists. When the company hired a special group of individuals who scored high on optimism but failed the normal screening, they outsold the pessimists by 21 percent in their first year and 57 percent in the second.

Self-worth deficit is a symptom of learned helplessness with characteristics that include: passivity, cognitive deficits, sadness, hostility, anxiety, loss of appetite, sleep loss, and norepinephrine and seratonin depletion. The treatment for learned helplessness is to change the individual's beliefs that they cannot change their own environment (Peterson, Maier, & Seligman, 1993). The key element is choice. Bredekamp & Copple (1997) suggested the developmentally appropriate classroom situation to create positive, successful experiences that help children to develop positive self-esteem. Weikart's High/Scope Curriculum used choice theory as a means to give children a sense of self efficacy (Goffin & Wilson, 2001). Miller (2000) concluded that feelings of self-worth make it possible for a child to learn acceptable behavior. Piaget discussed the movement of the child from the egocentric preschool years to the sociocentric primary years when they begin to understand themselves in relation to their peers. Children can become "calm, cooperative, and curious learners" only after their emotional needs have been met (p. 223).

The work of Kohlberg and Turiel in the area of moral development is related to the Piagetian contructivist-humanistic-affective educational methods. Moral development occurs in stages within interrelated domains in a similar way that Jean Piaget had described cognitive growth. Jean Piaget, the father of the constructivist approach, began observations of children's moral development in 1932. Kohlberg used Piaget's concept of egocentric thought in young children and extended the moral paradigm into six stages of growth which has been the basis of much of the character training that has become the conservative political rage of the present. An important common element of Kohlberg and Piaget' work is that morality is not taught by stories and parables but rather by experiential methods. McCown (1979) notes that experiential learning is another essential element in an emotional intelligence curriculum. The concepts involved in moral development that were once taught by the family and church have slowly been delegated to educators (Power, Higgins, & Kohlberg, 1989).

Learned helplessness could be considered the opposite of optimism. Consider this story:

> A man went to the zoo with his child. In the elephant section, there in open yard stood this multi-ton creature with not more than a kite string around his huge neck that was attached to a slight stick stuck loosely into the earth beside him and a small link chain placed lowly in front. The man complained bitterly to the attendant that the elephant could stampede and trample visitors without a proper restraint. The zoo keeper
> assured him everything was alright and explained, "When this jumbo was a little dumbo-baby they put him in that very spot with a thick iron chain around its neck that was attached to a heavy concrete post sunk deeply into the earth. In front of him was placed an electrified fence. Every time he attempted to advance forward he was heavily jolted. Years later all we need is a thin string attached to a stick and a small barrier to remind him. He doesn't believe he can ever move beyond that spot and with confidence we can say that he's going nowhere!"

Clearly, the elephant was a victim of learned helplessness. Children, too, can develop this condition when all decisions are made for them. They are told when to get up, what to do in school, when to go to the bathroom, when to eat, what to do when they get home, when to go to sleep. They soon discover that they have no control over their own lives.

When Salovey and Mayer coined the term emotional intelligence in 1990 (Salovey & Mayer, 1990), they were aware of the previous work on non-cognitive aspects of intelligence. They described emotional intelligence as a form of social intelligence that involves the ability to monitor one's own and others' feelings and emotions, to discriminate among them, and to use this information to guide one's thinking and action (Salovey & Mayer, 1990). Salovey and Mayer also initiated a research program intended to develop valid measures of emotional intelligence and to explore its significance. For instance, they found in one study that when a group of people saw an upsetting film, those who scored high on emotional clarity (which is the ability to identify and give a name to a mood that is being experienced) recovered more quickly (Salovey, Mayer, Goldman, Turvey, & Palfai, 1995). In another study, individuals who scored higher in the ability to perceive accurately, understand, and appraise others' emotions were better able to respond flexibly to changes in their social environments and build supportive social networks (Salovey, Bedell, Detweiler, & Mayer, 1999). In the early 1990's Daniel Goleman became aware of Salovey and Mayer's work, and this eventually led to his book, Emotional Intelligence. Goleman was a science writer for the New York Times, whose beat was brain and behavior research. He had been trained as a psychologist at Harvard where he worked with David McClelland, among others. McClelland (1973) was among a growing group of researchers who were becoming concerned with how little traditional tests of cognitive intelligence told us about what it takes to be successful in life.

Summary

To protect our future we need to create citizens who can adapt to a changing world. Our children need to learn to build new solutions to the new problems that arise in our global economy. Teaching emotional intelligence skills can lead to this type of citizen. We've learned that cognitive skills are predicated on emotional well-being. Emotional intelligence (EQ) has been proven to lead to successful academic and professional performance.

Chapter 2

The Role of Early Childhood Educators

Hernandez (1995) addressed the increasing depth and breadth in demands of early childhood educators to meet the needs of children. The ability of parents to meet the physical and affective needs of children is decreasing rapidly. Because of the rigorous demands of society, parents are often not only physically unavailable but alarmingly more frequently incapable of helping their children emotionally adapt to their reality. Institutions such as school and church are left to deal with these needs. Interestingly, the United States is the only country in the world that does not have either a religious context or a values program as a framework or foundation for its educational institutions. It is essential for schools to support the learning of parental and community values and the universal principles of society (McCown, 1998).

The decade beginning with 1990 saw the highest juvenile arrest rate for violent crimes: teens arrested for forcible rape doubled, teen murder rates quadrupled, teen suicide rates tripled as did the number of children under fourteen who were murder victims. Statistics for 1993 reported a drastic increase in the number of pregnant female children between the ages of ten to fourteen while the rates of venereal disease among teenagers tripled over the past twenty years. Heroin and cocaine use among white youth has climbed almost 300% when compared to rates in the 1970s and 1980s; drug abuse for the African-American youth has jumped to 13 times the rate of 20 years before. Educators may not be able to measure the effectiveness of affective educational techniques, but certainly this information is evidence of how purely cognitive methodology is not working. Goleman (1997) suggested that these statistics are warnings that society is headed for trouble.

Barr and Parrett (2001) reported that society is already in crisis and that prevention at the earliest possible developmental level is the cure; and they proposed that emotional development is the missing piece of the educational framework. Goleman (1997) suggested that educators care more about how well children read and write than "whether they will be alive next week" (p. 231). The recent emphasis on reading as the primary goal for educators may be counterproductive. Benchmarks for pre-kindergarten children in the state of Mississippi indicated that pre-kindergarten children should begin to separate reality from make believe (Thompson, Rucker, & Coleman-Potter, 2001). Conversely, Heidemann (1992) proposed that sociodramatic play is recognized as the highest level of dramatic play because it requires the combination of social and dramatic play skills. Sociodramatic play must include heavy elements of make-believe. It prepares a child for life's experiences. The representational skills practiced are essential to the child's ability to adapt to the give and take nature of social relationships. This element of growth has been totally ignored by the new Mississippi Early Learning Guidelines.

Governmental leaders function under the assumption that if children learn to read, then the emotional skills will follow (if they're even concerned about emotional skills at all). Educators and psychologists believe that the converse is true; reading skills are more easily assimilated when solid emotional skills are in place. Furthermore, emotional development has a greater bearing on success in today's world than does one's intelligence quotient (Goleman,1995). This is certainly true in the urban environment where guns and violence are part of everyday life with society losing teenagers by the minute to shootings and knifings (Barr and Parrett, 2001).

Over the last several decades, the central debate in the field of early-childhood education has been between one group that favors cognitive or preacademic approach to prekindergarten and kindergarten and another group that contends that the point of school in those early years is not to prepare for academic study; it is to allow children to explore the world, learn social skills and have free, unconstrained fun. The preacademic camp began to dominate the debate in the late 1980s, drawing on some emerging research that showed that children's abilities at the beginning of kindergarten were powerful predictors of later success. We have seen that this has not worked for our children.

More recently, though, a backlash has been growing against the preacademic approach among educators and child psychologists who argue that it misses the whole point of early-childhood education. "Kindergarten has ceased to be a garden of delight and has become a place of stress and distress," warned a report released in March by a research group called the Alliance for Childhood (2009), which is advised by some of the country's most esteemed progressive-education scholars. There is now too much testing and too little free time, the report argues, and kids are being forced to try to read before they are ready. The solution, according to the report's authors, is a return to ample doses of "unstructured play" in kindergarten. If kids are allowed to develop at their own paces, they will be happier and healthier and less stressed out. And there will still be plenty of time later on to learn how to read.

While many educators have theorized that emotional skills and social skills should be taught at home, others have argued that if children's parents were not taught emotional skills, they cannot teach them to their children. Educators have assumed if these parents have survived thus far, they must have some emotional skills. This is not necessarily so; they might have just been lucky (Goleman, 1995). Parents must be educated in the skills of emotional intelligence. Who, then, must take responsibility for teaching the skills necessary for a good, healthy life? The standards set forth by NAEYC clearly state that Early Childhood Educators must work with parents as well as children. With the proper emotional skills in place, teenage motherhood could certainly be curbed as children are taught healthy ways to channel emotions to avoid pre-marital sex. Drugs and violence could be avoided as an outlet for emotional well-being through a program teaching emotional intelligence. Barr and Parrett (2001) questioned the practice of providing children with cognitive skills when they have a great likelihood of growing up and getting shot, or making a rotten emotional decision and living a poor life.

We are left with our early childhood educators to help our children achieve the skills to become successful citizens in a democracy. Professionals in the field can use this valuable time between birth and age eight to teach children how to name and negotiate their feelings, to recognize the patterns of their feelings, to understand the consequences – both good and bad – of their feelings, and to navigate the feelings on which they focus. Early childhood is a time when children can develop intrinsic motivation, create an optimistic outlook on life, and become empathetic toward their peers. Many curricula use the tools of emotional intelligence to increase the EQ of children in their programs. We will look at a few of them in the following section.

Early Childhood Curricula that encourage the goals of Emotional Intelligence

Over the last few years, a new buzz phrase has emerged among scholars and scientists who study early-childhood development, a phrase that sounds more as if it belongs in the boardroom than the classroom: executive function. Originally a neuroscience term, it refers to the ability to think straight: to order your thoughts, to process information in a coherent way, to hold relevant details in your short-term memory, to avoid distractions and mental traps and focus on the task in front of you. And recently, cognitive psychologists have come to believe that executive function, and specifically the skill of self-regulation, might hold the answers to some of the most vexing questions in education today.

The ability of young children to control their emotional and cognitive impulses, it turns out, is a remarkably strong indicator of both short-term and long-term success, academic and otherwise. Self-regulation skills have been shown to predict academic achievement more reliably than I.Q. tests. The problem is that just as we're coming to understand the importance of self-regulation skills, those skills appear to be in short supply among young American children. Across the country, more than 5,000 children are expelled from pre-K programs because teachers feel unable to control them.

There is a popular belief that executive-function skills are fixed early on, a function of genes and parenting, and that other than medication, there's not much that teachers and professionals can do to affect children's impulsive behavior. In fact, though, there is growing evidence that the opposite is true, that executive-function skills are relatively malleable — quite possibly more malleable than I.Q., which is notoriously hard to increase over a sustained period. Tools of the Mind is a curriculum based on the teachings of Lev Vygotsky, a Russian psychologist who died of tuberculosis in 1934, at age 38. He believed that pretend play was a key to predicting later success in life.

Bodrova and Leong drew on research conducted by some of Vygotsky's followers that showed that children acting out a dramatic scene can control their impulses much better than they can in nonplay situations. In one experiment, 4-year-old children were first asked to stand still for as long as they could. They typically did not make it past a minute. But when the kids played a make-believe game in which they were guards at a factory, they were able to stand at attention for more than four minutes. In another experiment, prekindergarten-age children were asked to memorize a list of unrelated words. Then they played "grocery store" and were asked to memorize a similar list of words — this time, though, as a shopping list. In the play situation, on average, the children were able to remember twice as many words. Bodrova and Leong say they see the same effect in Tools of the Mind classrooms: when their students spend more time on dramatic play, not only does their level of self-control improve, but so do their language skills.

In the past, when psychologists (or parents or teachers or preachers) tried to improve children's self-control, they used the principles of behaviorism, reinforcing good and bad behaviors with rewards and punishments. The message to kids was that terrible things would happen if they didn't control their impulses, and the role of adults, whether parents or preschool teachers, was to train children by praising them for their positive self-control ("Look at how well Cindy is sitting!") and criticizing them for their lapses. And in most American prekindergartens and kindergartens, behaviorism, in some form, is still the dominant method. But Bodrova and Leong say that those "external reinforcement systems" create "other-directed regulation" — good behavior done not from some internal sense of control but for the approval of others, to avoid punishment or to win praise and treats. And that, they say, is a kind of regulation that is not particularly valuable or lasting. Children learn only how to be obedient, how to follow orders, not how to understand and regulate their own impulses. The goal is self-regulation (2007).

In the end, the most lasting effect of the Tools of the Mind studies may be to challenge some of our basic ideas about the boundary between work and play. Today, play is seen by most teachers and education scholars as a break from hard work or a reward for positive behaviors, not a place to work on cognitive skills. But in Tools of the Mind classrooms, that distinction disappears: work looks a lot like play, and play is treated more like work.

The Perry Project of the sixties used Piagetian pedagogy for urban preschoolers. The result of the project was the High-Scope curriculum. The program seeks to provide realistic experiential education. The curriculum is geared to the child's current stage of development to promote the spontaneous and constructive processes of learning and to broaden the child's emerging intellectual and social skills. (Morrison, 2001).

Weikart, in his HighScope Curriculum, created the subject of student control or choice theory in practice. In the eighties, William Glasser coined the term choice theory to discuss appreciating the consequences of our actions and that all behavior involves choice. (Glasser, 1988). As noted by Hohmann, Banet and Weikart (1979), in 1960, there were few clear guidelines on how to operate a nursery school (p.xii). Children received education through adult instruction organized by the teacher in skills deemed important to the teacher. Constructivist philosophy had not become acceptable in the early childhood arena. Still today, constructivist thought has not become the mainstream theory for educators.

The HighScope Curriculum is based on constructivist child development ideas in which children are viewed as active learners who learn best from activities they themselves plan, carry out and reflect upon. Adults observe, support, and extend the play of the children. Adults arrange interest areas in the learning environment, help to maintain a daily routine, and join in the activities by asking questions. The HighScope program is considered to be both child centered and teacher initiated in orientation (Goffin & Wilson, 2001).

The HighScope approach gives adults the tools they need to help children develop social abilities that contribute skills to solve problems without resorting to aggression or retreating into avoidance. Since early social and emotional experiences can shape the rest of a child's life, high-quality child care and preschool programs support and supplement family relationships. These early social experiences influence children's later ability to form satisfying relationships with family, friends, and workmates. The program emphasizes five major social learning areas. These are:
- Taking care of one's own needs

- Expressing feelings in words
- Building relationships with children and adults
- Creating and experiencing collaborative play
- Dealing with social conflict

The HighScope program uses a plan-do-review process to allow children to make choices in their activities. They offer the children time to evaluate the choices they made and then decide whether those choices worked out for them. In this way, children learn self-regulation skills that stay with them for the rest of their lives. Positive long-term effects have been documented with children from the Perry Project at 15 and 25 years. The children who attended Weikart's school were found to be better off economically, socially, and physically in both studies than children who attended ordinary preschools.

We know from research on the brain that the search for meaning is innate and this searching occurs through patterning. The arts offer a direct path to seeking patterns, layering experiences, and making meaning. Meaningful learning engages feelings, experiences, relationships, and the ability to see clearly with our eyes, hands, and bodies. Children become problem posers in art-rich environments. They call on their personal life of images and experiences to solve problems. Loris Malaguzzi says, "What children learn does not follow as an automatic result from what is taught, rather, it is in large part due to the children's own doing, as a consequence of their activities and our resources." (2005, p.64) The answer to the question, "What color is this?" or "How does this animal move?" is not moment specific, but tied to their whole life as a learner in the world. Becoming better readers and writers, understanding numbers, forming successful personal relationships involves putting many things together, layering experiences to solve word, number, or people problems. Reggio Emelia, an arts focused, project (*progettazione*) based program, is such a curriculum. Basically, the program involves four focus projects:

- Project Themes – This is the foundation, projects that all children do in the course of the program. They are arts based and meant to help children find the means to express themselves artistically.
- Environmental Projects – These are projects that grow out of the classroom areas.
- Daily Life Projects – These are projects that spontaneously emerge during daily life at school.
- Self-Managed Projects – These are projects set up for the children to do independently, alone or with a friend.

Teachers begin with young children of three years old and take their cues from the actions and discussions of the children to lead them on the path to discover themselves and the world around them. Children learn cognitive skills but also soon learn that that each child is important, respected, and valued. The teachers use questioning strategies to allow the children to reflect on, evaluate, and find solutions to everyday problems. They use morning meetings to discuss problems and solutions with the group. The Reggio process is, indeed, a form of self-science.

Finally, the National Association for the Education of Young Children (NAEYC,2009) suggested developmentally appropriate practice (DAP) as a means to reduce stress and create choices for young children. DAP is not a curriculum but a set of suggestions that create an environment for young children that leads to safe physical, emotional, social, and cognitive success. Even though these practices are not yet the norm and not all parties agree on the value of developmentally appropriate practice, the professionals in education should try to make parents and policy makers aware that a major cause of stress in children (especially lower socio-economic strata) is pushing the academics on children who are not yet ready for them. Further, the positive climate created by developmentally appropriate practice contributes to healthy emotional development. Child initiated environments empower children and reduce learned helplessness. The National Association for the Education of Young Children (NAEYC) believes that the application of the principles of developmentally appropriate practice can make a difference throughout a person's life. (Dunn, 1997, Bredekamp and Copple, 1997).

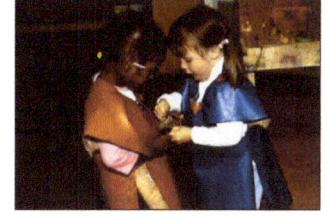

General Roles of Early Childhood Educators

The many ideas, quotes, thoughts, activities, and self questioning in Part II will help educators and parents work with young children within any academic curriculum to impart the constructs and skills of Emotional Intelligence (EQ). However, we will cover some important areas for teachers of young children to consider.

A. Create an environment that encourages self-regulation.

The impact of the environment on young children is too often underrated. Our goals as early childhood educators are to promote children's positive self-images, self-regulation, self-direction and a joy in learning. The physical arrangement of the classroom can do this if you keep the children in mind when you arrange your physical environment.

- Maintain clear physical boundaries to allow children to comprehend what boundaries are used for. They prevent intrusion into other children's space, and they provide structure and clear pathways for children to move throughout the room.
- Eliminate large open spaces and eliminate long pathways that might encourage running or other dangerous activities. Use furnishings and low room dividers to create observable barriers to unsafe or intimidating activities.
- Separate noisy areas (blocks, dramatic play) from quiet areas (library, writing center).
- Set up messy activities near water sources and on harder surfaces.
- Be certain that materials are appropriate for the children in the room – both developmentally and age appropriate. They should be challenging but not frustrating. (Beaty, 2008; Kostelnik, et. al., 2010)
- Manipulatives should be in good working order with no broken or missing pieces. To insure that your materials are together, keep a "missing piece cup" on a shelf where the children can place unknown pieces they find on the floor or tables. Take time each week to put things back together.

- All areas must be kept free of germs. Manipulatives need to be washed with a bleach mixture regularly.

> **Create Disequilibrium through Challenge:**
> It takes a moderate level of dissonance to learn and to gain new perspectives. Our job is to make it safe enough for people to go beyond comfort and conformity and to gently push them toward the land of the unknown. Your affect will influence this greatly -- if you quickly establish trust in the group, the exercise will give them a new and valuable perspective on themselves and their work.

- Keep materials stored so that they can be reached easily and independently by young children.
- When you notice children having difficulties or trying to solve puzzling problems, don't jump in right away to help them work out solutions. Observe, take note of how they approach the problems, and let them work things out on their own. Then use questions to help them see what they did.
- Provide quantities and space appropriate to the age and number of children in the group. An early childhood program serving children between 3 and 5 years of age should plan on having 40 to 60 square feet per child. Research shows that where there is a density of children and a little room or not enough materials for the number of children in a room, there is often an increase in the negative and idle behavior (Taylor, 2002).

B. Choice

Many teachers of young children do not use center time as a time for children to make choices. They divide the children into groups and rotate them throughout the room allowing a certain amount of time at each center. This practice makes for a very organized, teacher directed activity period. It could be called small group interaction.

Unfortunately, the teacher directed small group interaction time does not allow for choices. Center time is a time for children to make decisions on what interests them. Call it "Choice Time." It can be a time for children to take risks. They can try new things with the encouragement of the teacher. Here is where children find out about themselves and other children.

The time allotted to choice time should be just a little longer than may be comfortable for the teacher. Ask ourselves where we have to go. What is our hurry? Children need time to try something, put it away, and then try something else. Teachers should be participating through observation and asking open ended questions. Choice time is also when the teacher is given the opportunity to learn about the children in the classroom. The teacher should make careful notes about which centers interest each child. We use the child's interests and intelligence areas to not only increase each child's abilities in that particular area, but also to use that interest to create interest in other areas.

> **Many Ways to be Smart:**
> People learn in a variety of ways, and we need to teach to many learning styles. We also need to adapt and flex to effectively work with the complexities of real people.
>
> *In action:* Engage many different learning styles so different people can learn in their own best ways. In each conclusion, participants are encouraged to do their own synthesis and craft their own authentic next steps.

Encourage self-regulation skills through limiting the number of children in any particular center by giving each child a name tag and labeling each center with a number of symbols to represent the maximum number of children to occupy that space. An example of a symbol would be a construction hat for the block area, a book for the library/reading area, or a pencil for the writing area. The children, then, can place their nametag over the picture until they have completed their task. When they are finished, they can move to another area. Newcomers can either make a deal to trade places with children at a center or move on to another center.

You will find that children are more likely to remain interested and active in a task for longer periods of time when they are given real choices about materials to use. Children are also more likely to become self-directed if they can make real choices. Remember, the classroom belongs to the children (Beaty, 2008).

> **Inner Knowledge:**
> Our job is to create an environment/experience where children can find their own answers. Self-reflection is key!
>
> *In action:* Provide time and space for reflection. Share your own reflection. Validate answers -- focus on the deeper concepts vs. "right answers." Ask open ended questions.

Children may use manipulatives in ways that YOU did not have in mind. This experimentatation process is called self-discovery. Children learn through play. It is a natural process. Young children play with objects in the classroom in various ways. They may create ways to learn from the materials in your classroom that the teacher never considered. Let them. They may need to try different ways of looking at the computer keyboard until they see their effect on the screen. Boys may play with baby dolls in the way that they see their mother holding their baby brother. This is the way that they learn.

> **Process not product:**
> Learning comes from experiencing and reflecting -- doing, thinking, and feeling. Our job is to model appropriate thinking, actions, and behaviors.
>
> ***In action:*** *Use an experiential approach with many opportunities for discovery -- as well as powerful conceptual theories. Facilitators will be most successful if they model appropriate styles in setting up and debriefing the process.*

Young children do not learn numeracy, literacy, and emotional skills by sitting down and listening to the teacher. They need objects in the room to manipulate, to compare, to analyze, to classify, and to weigh. Children need opportunities to listen, to observe, to touch, and to organize in their own way. Children need to play. Because play has little to do with learning for most adults, we tend to feel the same about play for children. We are wrong. The wise teacher of young children will set up the room so that children can spend the majority of their time teaching themselves through play. Teachers can then observe, clarify, and remember (or make notes about) what the children do to assess learning styles, intelligence areas, and interests, as well as academic progress.

C. Identifying and Expressing Emotions – emotional literacy

My most gratifying moment as a Kindergarten teacher came when a young boy said to me, "I'm jealous." When I asked him why, he told me that the playdoh area was full and that he wanted to play there. We then went over to the area and negotiated a space for him.

Much will be covered in Part II in the area of thinking about and teaching the skills of emotional literacy. In Appendix A, you will find an exhaustive list of feelings words. The list on the right contains the eight constructs of emotional intelligence. To review, the first two comprise the area of knowing one's self. The next four are a matter of choice. Then, we move into the realm of giving one's self to make our world a better place in which to live. All of these begin in early childhood, while we continue to grow as we move through life. The choices we make

- Enhancement of emotional literacy
- Recognizing patterns of behavior
- Applying consequential thinking
- Navigating emotions
- Engaging intrinsic motivation
- Exercising optimism
- Increasing empathy
- Pursuing noble goals.

become harder and more expensive – emotionally, financially, salubriously, and academically.

As teachers of young children, we know that the children come to us with many unique and varied experiences – some good and some not-so-good. Some parents talk <u>with</u> their children about the things that happen to them, others talk only <u>to</u> their children, and some say very few words to the children at all (Fish, 2008; Hart & Risley, 2002). Thus, many young children may lack the words to express their own feelings and those of others. As early childhood educators, we need to help the children clarify these feelings. Emotional literacy could be considered a prerequisite to self-regulation. Another word for self-regulation is emotional regulation. The children learn how to understand themselves and others. They are then ready for successful interpersonal interactions, making good choices, problem solving, and learning how to learn.

> **Self-awareness:** The ability to understand one's self—thoughts, feelings, and behaviors.

Over the last decade, we have seen that reading is being stressed and tested, retested, and then tested some more in our classrooms. Some school districts have even begun basing teacher's salaries on the results of these tests. So why not use literature as a means to help children begin to understand emotion? Through reading and acting out stories, children can learn how other people handle their feelings, what happens when they handle them poorly, how they can successfully deal with problems, recognizing patterns of behavior in characters in a story, and the consequences of the characters' actions.

> **Emotional Literacy:** The ability to know words and concepts for negotiating emotions.

We will learn more about using literature with families and young children in Chapter 4. Now, we will examine some of the positive effects of teaching emotional intelligence skills.

Results of teaching emotional intelligence skills

Jensen (1998) made many practical suggestions for reducing stress and encouraging positive decision making skills. Conflict resolution skills are ways to seek positive natural opiate flow through the body to reduce violent tendencies. Hawkins & Catalano (1992) delineated the methodology of empowerment, choice, and cooperation. Teachers of children in his paradigm are taught strategies to maximize the time students are actually involved in activities, to break objectives into small easily attainable steps, and to provide motivation and incentives for effective teamwork. This approach has led to greater involvement and success for all students. We will see in the following sections that children are positively affected by interventions designed to teach the skills of Emotional Intelligence (EQ).

To address student improvement, the Six Seconds organization conducted a study of 13 different classrooms for six weeks; prior to the start, students completed an assessment, then had six lessons, then another assessment. While the data suggests that EQ training would be most effective with a longer period of training, results show that students' EQ increased significantly with even relatively brief exposure to the program (Freedman, 2003).

This finding led Reuven Bar-On (2005) to write: "At the end of the first year, the children were better able to understand and express themselves, to understand and relate with others, to manage and control their emotions, and to adapt to their immediate school environment. These important changes suggest that this program is viable." (p. 3).

EQ and Academic Achievement

The research into Emotional Intelligence (EQ) training and social-emotional learning curricula over the last 15 years has shown that intervention at all levels from preschool though adulthood brings about long-term, positive results. So far, the results indicate that emotional intelligence has extraordinary potential as a mediator of positive school outcomes. For example, in a 2004 study of 667 high school students, James Parker and team gave students an emotional intelligence assessment and compared those scores to their year-end grades. EQ and academic performance were shown to be strongly related. Participants in the study were asked to complete an EQ inventory between the first and second semesters of the academic year. At the end of the year, each EQ response was matched with the student's final grade point average. Students were then divided into three groups based on their grade point"

> ...Social and emotional learning students have significantly better attendance records; their classroom behavior is more constructive and less often disruptive; they like school more; and they have better grade point averages. They are also less likely to be suspended or otherwise disciplined."
> (Shriver & Weissberg)

One hundred percent of the teachers reported that Emotional Intelligence training increases cooperation and improves classroom relationships. In addition, they agreed (92%) that the program helped:
- Increase student focus/attention
- Improve teacher/student relationships.

The teachers also agreed (77-85%) that it worked to:
- Improve student learning
- Enhance collaborative work
- Increase positive verbal statements
- Decrease "put downs" (negative verbal messages) between students.

Today, students are under a great deal of stress, which can easily derail them. Applying emotional intelligence skills appears to be an effective coping mechanism. For example, Petrides, Frederickson, and Furnham (2004) suggest that specific aspects of emotional intelligence may be especially important for students at risk. Specifically, their research suggests that students who struggle academically face even greater pressures than their peers. High EQ may serve to mediate, and thus dampen, the effects of associated stressors making all the difference between acceptable and unacceptable academic performance.

In parallel to an individual student's capacity to cope, the school environment likewise has a major affect on performance. When students feel a sense of belonging in a respectful environment, they are more free to focus on their academic work. One of the ways emotional intelligence programs seem to improve academic achievement is by improving the school climate. Focusing attention on feelings and helping students and adults recognize the emotional impact of their choices may foster a more positive climate.

The Assessment of School Climate examines four aspects of the school climate: Empathy (feeling cared for), Accountability (sense of follow-through), Respect (considerate behavior), and Trust (belief in the people and institution). These factors are highly predictive of three critical outcomes:

- Connectedness,
- Learning, and
- Safety.

These outcomes are combined into a "School Performance" variable. Regression analysis finds that 62.36% of the variation in School Performance is predicted by the climate. More specifically, climate predicts:

- 47.92% of the variation in Connectedness
- 55.25% of the variation in Learning
- 37.30% of variation in Safety.

In summary, emotional intelligence is strongly linked to academic performance. High EQ seems to help children and youth manage the complexities and pressures that would otherwise deter their learning. This effect occurs both on an individual basis and in terms of the overall school climate. Among other noted benefits of emotional intelligence, studies suggest that students with higher emotional intelligence tend to demonstrate better school attendance than their classmates with lower EQ scores. Given the importance of staying in school both for academic and life success, the link between EQ and retention will be examined next.

EQ and Academic Retention

According to the United States Department of Education's Office of Educational Research and Improvement, 5% of high school sophomores, juniors, and seniors dropped out of high school in the 1999 school year (a rate that is consistent since the late 1980's). Furthermore, in 2000, nearly 11% of the 3.8 million 16- to 24-year olds in the US failed to earn a high school diploma.(Kaufman, Alt, Chapman, 2001).

Rumberger (1987) suggests that the personal consequences of dropping out of high school may include decreased economic benefit as a result of insufficient academic skill, as well as poorer psychological and physical health that arises as an indirect result of from employment and income challenges. The fact is school attrition hurts our students and our communities. Recent studies of EQ and college retention indicate that students with higher emotional intelligence are less likely to drop out of school than their peers.

Parker, Hogan, Eastabrook, Oke and Wood (2006) matched a sample of 213 individuals who had dropped out of their universities before the beginning of their second year with a group of 213 individuals who stayed with their academic programs. After accounting for age, gender, and ethnicity, results of the study suggested that the persistent group had significantly higher levels of EQ, interpersonal competency, adaptability, and stress management than students who withdrew from their programs.

Youth who do not complete high school are less likely to be employed than high school graduates (U.S. Department of Labor, 2003). Approximately 80% of prison inmates do not have a high school diploma (Office of Juvenile Justice and Delinquency Prevention, 1995).

EQ and Prevention

In addition to academic success and school retention, many studies have examined the relationship between emotional intelligence, health, and behavior. Daniel Goleman (1995) wrote about two model social emotional learning (SEL) programs; one is called Self-Science. Goleman asserted that EQ education is a critical component for improving life-outcomes: "Self-Science is an almost point-for-point match with the ingredients of emotional intelligence – and with the core skills recommended as primary prevention for the range of pitfalls threatening children." (p. 123). Studies now document this link, showing how developing emotional competence reduces risky behaviors (such as drug use, dropping out, and violence) while increasing pro-social behaviors (such as exercise, positive peer relationships, and leadership). As mentioned above, the Self-Science (Freedman, 2003) and Durlak & Weissberg (2005) studies found emotional intelligence programs improved student behavior. Likewise the retention data indicates high emotional intelligence may help youth mitigate stressors that could lead them to drop out of school. Perhaps this same capacity helps people avoid other risky behaviors.

The pro-social benefits of emotional intelligence begin at a very young age. In a study of four-year-olds, fifty-one preschoolers were observed, tracking how they behaved and how they were accepted by peers. Then they were tested to see how much knowledge they had about emotions (emotional literacy). Those with higher emotional knowledge were less involved in aggressive interactions and more accepted by their peers (Arsenio, Cooperman, & Lover, 2000).

This trend continues in elementary school. In a study of 160 students (mean age 10.8), those with higher EQ scores were recognized by teachers and peers both as cooperative and as leaders, and for being neither disruptive nor aggressive (Petrides, Sangareau, Furnham, & Frederickson, 2006). By middle school, the challenges become more severe, with middle schoolers experimenting with many risky behaviors including using alcohol or tobacco. Trinidad and Johnson (2002) assessed 205 middle school students in southern California, measuring both emotional intelligence and use of alcohol and tobacco. The teens with higher emotional intelligence were less likely to use alcohol and tobacco.

Carina Fiedeldey-van Dijk and the Six Seconds group (2007) assessed an international sample of 2,665 youth ages 7-18. The study compared scores on the Six Seconds Emotional Intelligence Assessment (SEI) – Youth Version with a composite "Barometer of Life" comprised of Good Health, Relationship Quality, Life Satisfaction, Personal Achievement, and Self-Efficacy. The graph below shows the positive correlation between the two measures.

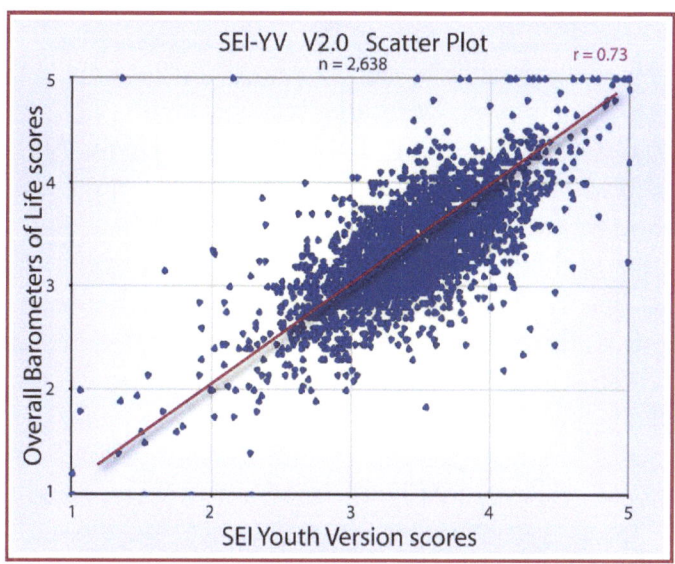

Youth EQ scores are strongly correlated with scores on important life outcomes (a composite of health, relationships, satisfaction, achievement, and efficacy).

Documentation that EQ training in the early years has long-term effects was demonstrated through a study involving 598 children from 15 Seattle schools. The intervention involved teachers, students and their parents. Teachers were given training in classroom management and strategies for instruction. Children were taught impulse control, how to get what they want without aggressive behavior, how to recognize the feelings of other people and how to stay out of trouble and still have a good time. Parents were taught family management skills, how to involve children in setting family rules, how to use positive reinforcement and how to better monitor their children.

The participants were divided into three groups. One group of 146 students received the intervention in grades one through six. A second group of 251 students received a partial intervention only in the fifth and sixth grades and the third group of 201 children was not exposed to the program.

Those people who received the full intervention in grades one through six showed the strongest effects and the most positive functioning in young adulthood. A dose effect noted from the intervention when participants were younger was evident. Those who received the partial intervention showed lesser effects, though they fared somewhat better than people who did not receive either intervention. The study also showed those who received the full intervention had significantly fewer lifetime sexually transmitted diseases. This finding relates to earlier results from the Seattle Social Development Project that showed children who received the full intervention started having sex later, had fewer sex partners and used condoms more consistently when they were teenagers.

On the economic front, the full-intervention group reported higher income, increased responsibilities at work and more community involvement. The study documented long-term effects on economic, sexual and mental health. The full-intervention group reported higher income, increased responsibilities at work and more community involvement. However, the full intervention had no effect on reducing substance use or cutting criminal behavior in young adulthood.

The intervention involved teachers, students and their parents. Teachers were given training in classroom management and strategies for instruction. Children were taught impulse control, how to get what they want without aggressive behavior, how to recognize the feelings of other people and how to stay out of trouble and still have a good time. Parents were taught family management skills, how to involve children in setting family rules, how to use positive reinforcement and how to better monitor their children.

The young adults surveyed in this study were evenly split between males and females. Forty-six percent were white, 26 percent black, 22 percent Asian-American and 6 percent Native American. The data, collected when the participants were 24 and 27 years old, came from the ongoing Seattle Social Development Project that followed a group of people from childhood into adulthood. The intervention affected developmentally important outcomes that change as people age. The study also showed those who received the full intervention had significantly fewer lifetime sexually transmitted diseases. This finding relates to earlier results from the Seattle Social Development Project that showed children who received the full intervention started having sex later, had fewer sex partners and used condoms more consistently when they were teenagers.

The effects of working with children in elementary school show up in their teen years as their rates of violence, heavy alcohol use and dropping out of school are reduced. By age 21 more of them have completed high school and have better jobs. And by ages 24 and 27 they are above the median in socio-economic status and education and they have less mental health and sexual health problems. Thus, we have documented long-term effects on economic, sexual and mental health from ensuring that urban teachers have the tools to teach the diversity of students they encounter and parents have the skills to raise kids in the complex world in which we live. (Hawkins, Kosterman, Catalano, Hill, Abbott, 2008).

In a study of teenage behavior, Mayer, Perkins, Caruso, and Salovey (2001) tested adolescents for Emotional Intelligence and verbal IQ. The teens were asked to think about the last time they were out with some friends and they wanted to do something they were uncomfortable with (e.g., it seemed risky or not a good choice. The responses illustrated that increased emotional intelligence helps teenagers make more complex, sophisticated, and pro-social decisions.

There are several EQ studies with college students that reinforce the data presented above. Marc Brackett and team have conducted studies on self-care, found significant correlations between low EI and negative behaviors (e.g., use of drugs and alcohol, violence, vandalism), especially for males. (Brackett, Mayer, & Warner, 2004).

It is becoming clear that the real value in following people over time is that we get to see how what we do in childhood affects adult lives and has enduring effects as they change. We need to know how one phase of development affects the next step, so we need more studies that follow people over time. We find many studies that link emotional intelligence skills and life outcomes, but we cannot always attribute how these skills were acquired.

For instance, there are numerous studies of emotional intelligence and positive life outcomes in adults. For example, a study of 365 students and adults in Greece (mean age 25) found a strong correlation between EQ and issues with anxiety and with overall health. (Tsaousis & Nikolaou,.2005).

Six Seconds' researchers had 665 adults complete the Six Seconds Emotional Intelligence Assessment (SEI) and a questionnaire about success factors. The success factor questionnaire included items about health, quality of life, effectiveness, and relationships – outcomes combined into a Life Success variable. Regression analysis revealed a strong relationship: 54.79% of variation in Life Success is explained by scores on the SEI. People with higher emotional intelligence also tend to score higher on success factors including health, relationships, quality of life, and effectiveness (Freedman, Ghini & Fieldeldey-van Dijk, 2006).

Summary

We have seen that the emphasis on cognitive development in the early years has not proven to be effective in creating optimistic, productive young adults. The results of this technique have proven disastrous for many adolescents. The earlier programs of the sixties – HighScope (the Perry Project), Reggio Emelia, and Self-Science – have proven to have positive results with our children over time. Why, then, have we moved back toward an emphasis on the cognitive in the last 30 years? We cannot answer this question, but we can advocate for a larger emphasis on social/emotional skills for the future. In the next chapter, we will look at the effects on the brain and how the wiring of the brain can empower our children with the tools to create a better world.

Chapter 3

Changing Brain Physiology Though Affective Education

Three discoveries have led to the recognition of emotions as an entirely new neuroscience discipline: emotions have physical pathways and priorities, brain chemicals involve emotions, and there is a link between these pathways with learning and memory.

Studies have identified specific sites in the mid-brain where fear or pleasure activates specific neurons that respond to these emotions from the thalamus to the amygdala which exerts tremendous influence on the cortex. Communication flows between the amygdala and the cortex with more feedback from the amygdala. This design of the feedback circuit ensures that the impact of emotion will usually be greater. Brain chemicals are transmitted and dispersed to wide areas of the brain and body by message molecules or peptides. Therefore, chemicals produced from emotions influence all behavior (Goleman,1995; Davidson & Sutton, 1995). Ninety-eight percent of all communication within the body is through peptide messengers (commonly known as gut feelings) which implies a far greater role for the understanding and integration of emotions in the learning process (Pert, 1997).

Affective growth and actual documentation of the effects of experiential life on the physical brain have been addressed through methods such as positron emission tomography (PET) scans. The neurolinguistic programming methods (NLP) used by psychologists in the 1970's has been improved. Scientists can now document what is going on in brains. Magnetic resonance imaging (MRI) can be used to study delayed language development. Pictures of brain development show that experiences in prenatal through early childhood periods have most certain effects on the development of speech patterns, as well as individuals' perceptions of what is safe, attainable, challenging, and rewarding (Kotulak,1997).

Wolfe (2001) noted that the reticular activation system in the hypothalamus is the gate to higher level thinking. Children with emotional problems cannot achieve high level cognition because the gate remains closed, and they continue to function in the lower level emotional state of the amygdala where emotions first develop. As self-awareness and emotional intelligence develops, thoughts are allowed to move freely up to the thalamus and the parietal lobes and back to the amygdala giving freedom to choose how to deal with experiential life. We call this movement "navigating emotions." McCown (1978) considered affective awareness to be a major contributing factor to cognitive growth. Freedman (2001) expressed pleasure at seeing the age old truths of confluent growth being confirmed by specialized and technical brain research.

Jensen (1998) used the latest brain pictures to help teachers and parents understand the impact of this research on education. Emphasis was placed on understanding the development of the thalamus, which controls what a learner perceives to be rewarding, and the hippocampus, which serves as an inhibitor to help the individual sort out what is important and what is not important. Physiological impacts at the prenatal stage can negatively affect young children through adulthood, unless intervention takes place. Barr and Parrett (2001) emphasized that the earlier problems are recognized and remediation begun, the better the opportunity for the children's emotional adjustment. We saw in the last chapter how early intervention can last a lifetime.

Since children's emotional education begins before birth, knowledgeable parents express support of the attitude of caring with direct consequences for a growing fetus. The most rapid pace of brain development occurs during the prenatal months. Thus, a stressful pregnancy can create cognitive, motor, and emotional problems later (Kotulak, 1997). Parents who plan for the birth of a child by observing good prenatal practices or changing the home environment in preparation for the new life to enter the household have already established an empathetic attitude for the child. Non-stressful birthing techniques offer opportunities to reduce tension from the very beginning of life outside the womb (Coles, 1997).

Conversely, the potentially damaging effects of adult stress can also be transferred to newborns. Infants born to mothers who are suffering from major depression tend to have lower electrical activity in brain areas that regulate joy, happiness, curiosity, and other positive emotions. The connections between brain cells will not be reinforced if the child continues to do without the proper emotional input. More stress can create more cortisol which can lead to a smaller hippocampus. The infant brain then lacks the necessary signals to wire its positive emotional neural networks (Kotulak, 1997).

During the first 36 months of life, the brain is wiring itself to communicate with the rest of the body. Ledoux (1996) stated that it is not only the brain that affects cognitive and emotional growth, but also the communication between the brain and the rest of the body. It was formerly assumed that synapse was the only chemical that made animals react; today, medical professionals recognize that other chemicals involved in synapse such as seratonin, dopamine, and cortisol communicate with other parts of the body via peptides. Jensen (1998) refers to these peptides as the body's "emotional highway" (p. 75).

Goleman (1995) suggested that emotional balance (or emotion quotient – EQ) has a greater bearing on success in today's world than does the Intelligence Quotient. Jensen (1998) cited that an analysis of emotional balance in reference to fetal and infant brain chemistry indicated that: "...[between] 0 and 18 months ... [infants need]... loving care, laughter, smiles...[parents should] bond with [the] child to avoid threats" (p. 86).

Caregivers have classified infant emotional behavior prior to six months of age or [before] language development. Babies are described as bossy, temperamental, good natured, or easy to get along with. Izard & Read (1986) developed an emotional measurement scale used by many scientists to identify the affective states of infants and toddlers. This scale has been used to rate both the central nervous system and the autonomic nervous system responses to various stimuli in infants. Test results using these scales have validated the work of Piaget and Erikson.

Erikson (1959) described conflict resolution or crisis dichotomy behaviors in terms of "oral reassurance" (p. 65). The initial balance between basic trust vs. basic mistrust does not seem to be related to the amount of food or demonstrations of love from the caregiver but to the quality of the parental relationship. The successful balance of trust is thought to translate into adults who are "...less dependent on mild or malignant forms of addiction, on self delusion, and on avaricious appropriation" (p. 64).

Ramey and Ramey (1999) maintain that infants cannot be given too much attention. Often well-meaning intellectual parents, who believe that their child should never have to cry to get to have needs met, misinterpret this trust issue. Similarly, these same informed parents want to force feed knowledge into their children at a young age because the brain is wiring itself so rapidly. Neither of these concepts are accurate. Research has shown that challenge creates growth; an infant's cry is its way of communicating needs. Secondly, putting this same infant in an inappropriate learning situation causes stress, which hinders emotional development (Jensen, 1998).

Kagan's (1992) study of middle-class preschool children indicated that one in three had psychological problems primarily related to a negative environment. He said that the causes are always in the biology of the child, either a certain inherited neuro-chemistry, structural abnormalities that occurred prenatally, or a bad environment. The bad environment--strife at home, abuse, bad peers, and lack of role models--is always the most prevalent cause. (Kotulak, 1997).

Children who manipulate their environments to be fed or kept warm are experiencing internal rewards. Using the research on brain chemistry, it was suggested that the brain makes its own rewards for the body. These rewards are called opiates and they are generated in the thalamus. They are like natural high inducing drugs. Seratonin and dopamine are two natural opiates. Different children receive external rewards in different ways. As noted by (Jensen, 1998):

> The brain's internal reward system varies from one [child] to the next. You'd never be able to have a fair system. How students respond depends on genetics, their particular brain chemistry, and life experiences that have wired their brains in a unique way. Rewards work as a complex system of neurotransmitters binding to receptor cites on neurons. These sites act like ports for the docking of ships. Here, the neurotransmitters will either deliver an excitatory message to a ... receptor site or an inhibitory message to a receptor. Without these switches in the brain ... all life experiences would [be] the same... That makes rewards unequal from the start. (p. 66)

Study of Erikson's dichotomy indicate that although infants are rewarded internally by the response of caregivers, little is known about what triggered the child's internal reward system until later in life. During Erikson's second crisis, autonomy vs. shame and doubt, children are learning to control their physical body with potty training being an obvious issue. Researchers have now determined that during this stage of development one of three chemicals seratonin, cortisol, or dopamine produces change to receptor cites in the brain during exposure to trauma.

The issue of control is at the heart of what is called learned helplessness. Emotional responses vary from anxiety to anger to depression. People who were stimulated to helplessness often become anxious, depressed and restless. Research findings reported that exposure to helplessness increased a liking for hostility; when an individual perceives that he is threatened for a period of time, he will choose to strike out against others who he might believe to be the oppressors (Trice, 1982, Jensen, 1998, Kotulak, 1996). Hence, we find the rebellious attitudes of many adolescents.

Once again, brain development is affected by the child's environment. Just like the thalamus generates the rewarding chemicals, the hippocampus acts like an inhibitor to help the individual sort out what is important and what is not important. When a child feels stress, the glands release a chemical (peptide) called cortisol . The body responds with cortisol whether it faces physical, environmental, academic, or emotional danger. According to one study, high cortisol levels lead to the death of brain cells in the hippocampus. These physiological impacts of stress occur from infancy through adulthood (Peterson et al., 1993, Kotulak, 1996, Jensen, 1998).

Conversely, Bluestein (2001) asks, "When we talk about stress in children's lives, what do we mean?" (p. 49). Stress could be anything that a child sees as a threat to survival or self-image. The result to the wiring of the brain is the same regardless of the cause. Sroufe (1986) emphasizes that the continued unfolding of the emotions is intrinsically linked with cognitive development. Most emotions require an understanding of the relationships with others. Some require a sense of self. Other emotions require a comparison of behavior with an internalized standard. For example, one cannot identify the feeling of shame until there is some sense of self-awareness. The development of aggression from object centered to person-centered changes as the child moves from the egocentric to the sociocentric stage. When children begin to comprehend that other people have points of view, they may develop either empathy or aggressive tendencies based on previous experiences.

Related to this development of aggression is, again, Seligman's (1993) learned helplessness which begins at the early stages of development, but continues throughout life. Often people decide that they cannot change unhealthy behavior because they believe that they are stuck in a rut. People believe that they are in this unbeatable rut because they have learned that they are helpless and must live with their hopeless misery. Changes in the wiring of the brain occur throughout life. The changes can be negative or positive. Kotulak (1996), Sroufe (1986), Caine & Caine (1997) and others agree that growth in the brain is environmentally based. Gazzaniga (1988) cites a study that found atrophy levels in the hippocampus of Vietnam Veterans suffering from posttraumatic stress disorder. These levels were higher than the levels of the control group ($t = 16$ $p < .05$).

Kotulak (1996) noted that the first three years of a child's life are critically important to brain development and further stated that "...abuse, poverty, neglect, or sensory deprivation can reset the brain's chemistry in ways that make some genetically vulnerable children more prone to violence" (p. 86).

Some professionals believe that once the brain is wired towards violence or emotional negativity, intervention cannot change it. Kotulak (1996), Jensen (1998), McCown (1978, 1998) and others believe that a person's wiring can be changed through meaningful experiences to counteract the damage. A look at the recent research on violent behavior and brain wiring indicated that even though violent tendencies begin very early in life, they can be reversed through various programs focusing on emotional intelligence.

On the subject of learned helplessness, Jensen (1998) cited animal experiment on the subject of rewiring the brain. A series of animal experiments illuminated the seriousness of lack of control. Dogs were placed in separate cages. They were given mild shocks through the grid floor, with no chance to escape. After their resignation became chronic, the shock was eliminated on half the cage. The dog was then dragged across to the safe area to let it feel the altered grid and see the light indicating safety. But the dog went right back to the shocked side and curled up in fear again. This is similar to a student who has learned to fail and simply won't even try. Students who have learned to be helpless may need dozens of positive choice trials before becoming mobilized again. The brain must rewire itself to change the behavior (Peterson, et al., 1993).

Amazingly, a single exposure to trauma can produce changes to receptor sites in the brain. Remember, though, it's the issue of control, which is at the heart of learned helplessness, which has powerful biological consequences. If the student is in a traumatic situation and he makes choices, the condition will not occur, regardless of the outcome. This may be why, time and again, educational reformists have pushed the notion of student control, choice, or child-centered activities. At a typical school, nearly every decision, from length of time on learning to whom to work with, is dictated and managed outside student control (Gazzaniga, 1988).

Brain based learning is a concept developed by Caine & Caine (1997). Their conclusions are drawn from many disciplines. Children are viewed as a dynamic entity composed of body, mind and brain. The authors list twelve brain/mind principles:

1. The brain is a complex adaptive system
2. The brain is a social organ.
3. Humans innately search for meaning in life.
4. Patterning is the method through which we search for meaning.
5. Emotions are a cornerstone to patterning.
6. Parts and wholes are perceived and created simultaneously.
7. There are two parts of learning—focus and peripheral attention.
8. Both conscious and unconscious processes are important to learning.
9. There is more than one way to organized memory.
10. Learning is developmental.
11. Threat inhibits learning and challenge enhances it.
12. Every brain is unique.

Feelings are different from Emotions

In everyday language we often use the terms "feeling" and "emotion" interchangeably. This shows how closely connected emotions are with feelings. But for neuroscience, emotions are more or less the complex reactions the body has to certain stimuli. When we are afraid of something, our hearts begin to race, our mouths become dry, our skin turns pale and our muscles contract. This emotional reaction occurs automatically and unconsciously. Feelings occur after we become aware in our brain of such physical changes; only then do we experience the feeling of fear.

Feelings are formed by emotions. As we will see in part II, emotions flow through our body in incredibly fast and in voluminous quantities. When we label an emotional response, we call it a feeling. Emotions alone--without conscious feelings--would not be enough. Adults would be as helpless as babies if they suddenly lost their sense of self. It is through learning about ourselves that we learn which feelings we focus on.

Consciousness, much like our feelings, is based on a representation of the body and how it changes when reacting to certain stimuli. Self-image would be unthinkable without this representation. Humans have developed a self-image mainly to establish a homeostatic organism. The brain constantly needs up-to-date information on the body's state to regulate all the processes that keep it alive. This is the only way the human organism can survive in an ever changing environment (Damasio, 2005).

Summary

Brain based learning involves both orchestrated immersion (teacher direction) and active processing of information (experiential base) to maximize learning. They insist on a state of relaxed alertness free from stress and ready to learn. They do not propose any single teaching method but promote a framework that will maximize the efforts of the teacher and student.

Raising Emotionally Intelligent Children

Chapter 4

Emotional Intelligence with families and educators

With mounting evidence that emotional intelligence programs improve school outcomes, several additional questions arise, including:

- How do we help parents improve their EQ?
- How does EQ help educators?

We now understand that people can improve their EQ skills beginning at the prenatal stage through octogenarians. We have seen that the earlier we begin working on these skills, the easier it is to gain them. People of any age are capable of change. Further, the more intensive the learning experience; the more effectively people can begin to apply their emotional intelligence skills.

Educational researchers know so much about how family situations affect children, but government policy and parental behavior does not seem to reflect this knowledge. A study, "The Family: America's Smallest School," conducted by the Educational Testing Services (ETS) suggests that a lot of problems have to do with what takes place in the home, the level of poverty, and government's inadequate support for programs that could make a difference – for instance high-quality day care and paid maternity leave (Barton & Coley, 2007).

The E.T.S. researchers took four variables that are beyond the control of schools: The percentage of children living with one parent; the percentage of eighth graders absent from school at least three times a month; the percentage of children 5 or younger whose parents read to them daily, and the percentage of eighth graders who watch five or more hours of TV a day. Using just those four variables, the researchers were able to predict each state's results on the federal eighth-grade reading test with impressive accuracy.

"Together, these four factors account for about two-thirds of the large differences among states," the report said. (p. 24). In other words, the states that had the lowest test scores tended to be those that had the highest percentages of children from single-parent families, eighth graders watching lots of TV and eighth graders absent a lot, and the lowest percentages of young children being read to regularly, regardless of what was going on in their schools.

We can see that children may already be far behind by the time they get to kindergarten because of family situations, and they tend to stay behind all through high school.

How to Help Parents and Families Improve their Emotional Intelligence

A study to understand how parents could be taught EQ skills, and how these skills would then affect their children was conducted by Sue McNamara (2006) in which she administered an interview and the SEI assessment, then delivered four weeks of parent education using the six-seconds "EQ for Families" program, and then followed-up with a post-interview and a repeat of the SEI assessment. Parents also kept a daily journal. Parents' scores increased significantly and according to their journals and exit interviews, family interactions became much more positive.

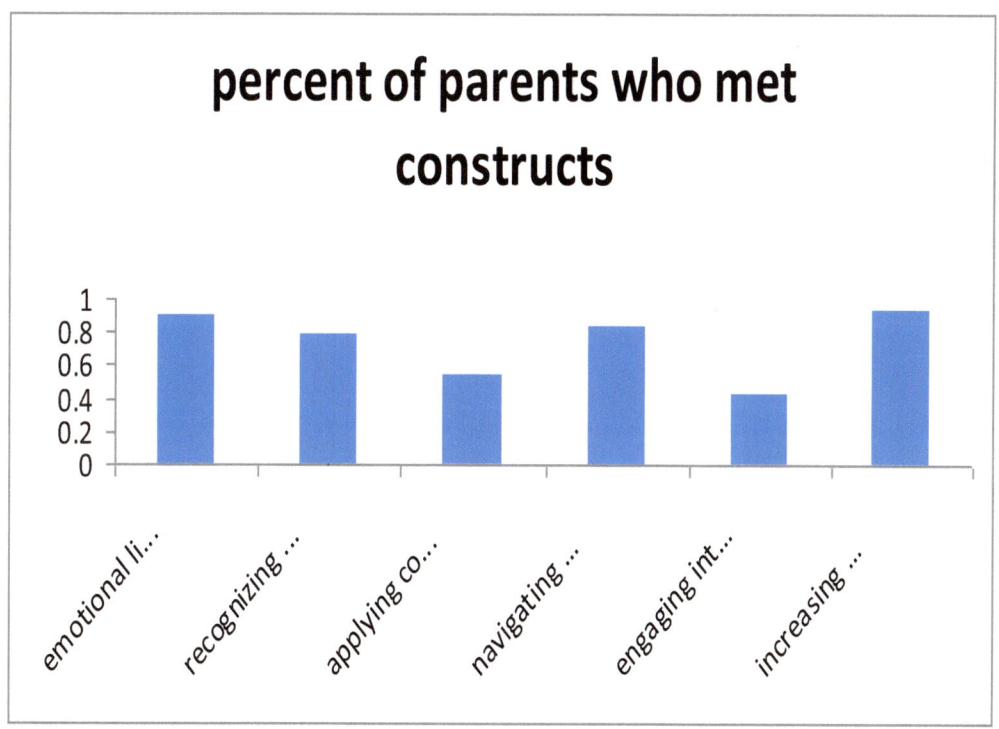

Six elements were measured during the program-emotional literacy, recognizing patterns of behavior, applying consequential thinking, engaging intrinsic motivation, and increasing optimism. 54.7% of the families met five of the six elements.

Families Uniting through Literature

Fish (2008) has tried several methods of working with families to encourage communication and emotionally intelligent behaviors. The investigator came to learn that the interventionists must also possess and recognize EQ skills in order to be effective instruments of change in the parents or caregivers. He trained graduate students and practicing teachers to act as emotional intelligence interventionists with children at risk between birth and seven years-old and their families in several studies of family EQ. The training sessions lasted for a minimum of two weeks up to eight weeks. He trained the interventionists in self-efficacy and eight elements of EQ:

1. Emotional literacy,
2. Discovering patterns of behavior,
3. Consequential thinking,
4. Emotional navigation,
5. Engaging intrinsic motivation,
6. Becoming optimistic,
7. Empathy, and
8. Goal setting for the common good.

The programs used literature and music (song and dance) dealing with these EQ themes. One of the bases for this program came from the work done by Hart and Risley

(2002) who found that parents of young children from lower income homes had much less conversation with their children than did parents in higher income homes. Earlier versions of the program proved unsuccessful because parents were not actively encouraged to participate in the reading comprehension and discussion of the themes of the books used. We found that the families were not reading and talking about the books at home. They were not engaged in the program. We therefore amended the program to focus on the parents of the children because research shows that parents are most effective in influencing the future academic and emotional responses of their children.

The goals of the program were:

- To encourage parents to spent more quality time with their children,
- To encourage parents to be responsive to their children's questions and concerns,
- To encourage parents to increase the quantity of words used in conversation, and
- To encourage parents to express approval/affirmation of children's thoughts and feelings.

Additionally, we planned to use the progress of this program to determine future methodology to help parents achieve the goals. The project investigator hypothesized that the most effective means for teaching parents these skills could be accomplished through the transmission of Emotional Intelligence (Literacy) skills both in groups and at the participants' homes. Two of the inventories given to the parents were the Parenting Styles Inventory and the Emotional Literacy Inventory. The purpose of these tests was to focus on the skills most needed by the caregivers of the children.

Additionally, between nine and twelve books were given to the children to take home and keep to begin a library of their own at home. Not only does ownership in a book create reading self-efficacy in the children, but the books also gave the parents motivation to join and remain in the program. The books were donated through the efforts of the First Book Campus Advisory Board, a student organization on the campus of a local university.

In our first session during 2007, we partnered with a summer program at an urban church. Masters candidates in the Families in a Cross-Cultural Perspective class acted as interventionists. There were 28 candidates in the class. Of these, only 24 were in a posture to act as interventionists. We had whole group sessions every Thursday evening at the church with the parents, children, and students for eight (8) weeks. The project investigator acted as facilitator and storyteller for the programs. Candidates were paired with families, and they were expected to meet away from the group at least once per week. Some parents of our candidates and the Chairman of the Department of Elementary and Early Childhood Education expressed concern for the candidates meeting in that particular area of the city – an urban, lower economic, higher crime neighborhood. We persevered, and the results were somewhat successful. Participant recruitment was easy since the church brought in the families. There was a question as to the participation of the candidates because some parents noted in their Post Program Inventories that they were never contacted by the interventionists (candidates). Upon reading the description portfolios of the candidates, the project investigator further noticed that some candidates did not comprehend the purpose and goals of the program. Many thought that their job was to work with the children of the family on phonics or other skill based reading problems.

The candidates who were responsible for the group programs, door prizes, and snacks did an excellent job. They were encouraged to seek donations for snacks and door prizes. When donations could not be found, the project investigator subsidized the necessary ingredients through his publishing company. Still, the candidates showed good planning and follow-through skills to make for successful sessions.

During this version of the project, we learned an important lesson regarding giving the books to the children. The investigator hired a project assistant who was responsible, among other things, for the dispersement of the books. During the first group session, she brought all of the books for the program into the hall. The families swarmed her to grab books for their children, nieces, nephews, and neighbors. We were forced to order more books to cover those lost for the completion of the project. We have never brought the entire supply of books to a program since then. Books are now given to the interventionists to take to the families.

The second rendition of the program during the fall of 2007 was entirely unsuccessful. The candidates were required to recruit families for the program. They were to bring them to the first session held at the Jackson State College of Education Building. Books were again donated by the First Book Campus Advisory Board for the participating families. Of the 29 students enrolled in the class, only one candidate successfully recruited a family and brought them to the session. After stern reprimand by the instructor (project investigator) and repeating the instructions to find students from their own schools or churches who were at risk to recruit, more students brought families to the second session. Unfortunately, the candidates brought their relatives, friends, or colleagues contrary to their instructions. Candidates who worked for the local public school district informed the project investigator that they were not allowed to bring students from their own schools because it was against the rules to meet with parents during off-hours. Snacks and door prizes were subsidized by the publishing company with only a few donations. Candidates were unable to successfully motivate parents and children at the group sessions with renditions of the books or discussions about the themes. The emotional intelligence component to the program was incomprehensible to the candidates. Through reading the visitation logs and family descriptions, it was determined that the majority of the candidates still interpreted the program as a reading skills program for the children. Even though Post Program Inventories were sent to the families, the inventories received were not usable since they were from friends, colleagues, or family of the candidates.

After reflection of the first and second programs, the investigator sought to revise some of the operational components to include funds from an outside source, hiring interventionists, the addition of a project coordinator to help train and supervise interventionists, recruitment, and other details, and the addition of a project assistant to keep track of records and data. The coordinator and assistant had both successfully completed the program as students. Funds were obtained through the gracious efforts of the Mississippi Learning Institute (MLI).

We sought to begin contacting parents prior to the end of the school term because we wanted to enlist the help of the teachers in contacting the parents. We began by contacting the principals at MLI schools to ask for lists of P - 1 children who were deemed "at risk" by their teachers or school literacy coaches. Two elementary schools responded. We then contacted other elementary schools because the Project Coordinator (PC) worked there formerly and/or knew the literacy coach. One other family was recruited by the PC because she thought that they needed and would benefit from the program. We then advertised for interventionists who had either completed the Families in a Cross-Cultural Perspective coursework or had experience working with families. We received seven replies and chose four who had the qualifications we desired.

From our list of 67 possible children, we were able to contact twenty (20) parents. Of these, sixteen (16) agreed to participate. After a brief (two week) training session with our interventionists, we began meeting with the families. Each interventionist worked with four (4) families. We decided to reduce the number of whole group sessions to three for the summer.

Our first family meetings were introductory. Then, the interventionists initiated the pre-program inventories, the release of liability and oral consent forms. Again, the books were donated through the generous support of the First Book Campus Advisory Board. The interventionists also gave the family and introduced the first books for the program – *The Talking Eggs* and *Mufaro's Beautiful Daughters*. These books were chosen because the themes were related to healthy goals and being comfortable in your own skin.

Our first group session in June was well attended. The project investigator acted as facilitator. He explained the program and introduced the staff, while the coordinator introduced the books and themes. Healthy snacks were served. Session evaluations were positive.

One family incident can be relayed here. A family who lived in the apartments across the street from the meeting place did not attend any sessions. The interventionist and the PC both encouraged the parent to bring the children to the event. The parent could not come because she complained that it was too far to walk, and she needed transportation.

The interventionists were instructed to give all initial paperwork to the PC or PA during the third week in June. Upon receipt of paperwork and monitoring by the PI, we had another staff meeting to clarify our goals. One of our interventionists and several parents were under the impression that we were to help children who were behind in their compartmentalized reading skill areas. The interventionists were told to recommend these families to the Reading Center at the local urban university. One such family could not find transportation to the center even though several suggestions were made. For liability reasons, our staff was unable to transport the families.

The interventionists continued visiting parents. We had a staff meeting where staff met candidates from the Families in Cross-Cultural Perspectives course Candidates accompanied interventionists and interviewed parents on their own during the last part of June and early July. We had another whole group session in late June. Attendance was not as high as the initial meeting. The same format as the initial meeting was followed, but candidates took a larger role in the presentations.

In mid-July, we had our final whole group session. It was poorly attended. Candidates from the graduate practicum course volunteered to present a resource fair to the families. They were also instructed to create helpful lesson plans for the interventionists to carry out with their families. Most of the material they created was useless because they were not familiar with the goals of EQ.

After the third meeting the program began to wind down with interventionists and candidates meeting with families to get and give feedback on the inventories, determine goals for the family after the program was over, listen to suggestions for program improvement, etc. We had a final debriefing meeting with the staff and the candidates during the last week in July. Much good feedback was given at the meeting.

We analyzed data from the inventories using simple statistics. Emotional Intelligence was measured with an investigator created version of the Parenting Styles Assessment. We have broken down the answers to the inventories given into six subsets. The chart at the beginning of this section shows that over half of the families met five of the six elements after the program. Post program interviews with parents showed that they were interested in learning more about EQ and emotion coaching parenting styles. The above competencies were demonstrated through the themes presented in the books given to the families. Each competency was addressed during the meetings with the families by the interventionists.

We have repeated the program twice during the last two years using graduate students as interventionists; each with greater success. A key element in the success of the program is the length of time that the interventionists were trained in the components of EQ. The book you are now reading was initially undertaken as a means to train these interventionists. This investigator will continue to improve on methods to work with parents to empower them with the emotional intelligence skills to raise families that make successful decisions and lead successful lives. Hopefully, we can decrease the gap that exists between young children from urban areas and their counterparts in the suburbs.

Helping Educators with EQ

In addition to the benefits to children and parents, developing emotional intelligence helps educators. For example, Stone, Parker, and Wood (2005) studied 464 principals and vice-principals in Ontario. They concluded that overall EQ was a significant predictor of administrative success. That is, educators with high EQ were more often rated as above average administrators by both supervisors and staff. The administrators who were rated "above average" also had a significantly higher level of EQ.

Bank Street College in New York City uses emotionally responsive practice to help teachers, administrators, clinicians, and support staff work together to ensure the emotional well-being of children in school by building on the well-documented connection between emotional wellness and learning potential. Emotionally responsive practice is a form of preventative mental health, as it promotes connection and decreases isolation that can put stressed children at risk as they grow older. They have shown that children of all ages need an atmosphere of warmth to thrive, and the warmth of close human contact.

Summary

It is clear that higher EQ leads to better learning, parenting, and teaching. In Part II, we will look at some ways to work with adults and children to increase their EQ.

Practical Ways to Teach and Think About Emotional Intelligence

IGNORED	LONELY	FRUSTRATED	OVERWHELMED	BASHFUL
UNHAPPY	EXCITED	KIND	ANGRY	MAD
PLAYFUL	SCARED	FREE	TIRED	CURIOUS
NAUGHTY	RESTLESS	QUITE SILLY	HAPPY	GLAD
WORRIED	ZANY	VICIOUS	DISCOURAGED	JOLLY

Part II

Raising Emotionally Intelligent Children:

Introduction to Emotional Intelligence

What is Emotional Intelligence?

It is a research-based set of skills that helps people make wise and empathetic decisions.

The process follows three steps:

- **Know Yourself**: Self-awareness. It helps people understand their own thoughts, feelings, and actions.

- **Choose Yourself**: Self-management. It helps people follow their intentions and live more consciously.

- **Give Yourself**: Self-direction. It helps people align their daily choices with their values and purpose so they act with integrity.

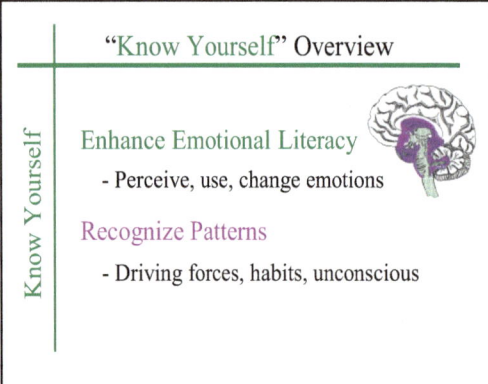

Once we learn about ourselves, we are opening the door to healthy choices. We begin to understand how our feelings are connected to our behavior.

For Parents and Teachers

For young children, knowing the emotions they are feeling, how to name those feelings and what they **do** about those feelings are the beginnings of emotional literacy. I require students in some of my courses to keep a "Feelings Journal" during the semester to help them get in touch with their own feelings. We also take several "feelings words" and discuss the meanings for grown-ups as well as children. Once we begin to recognize and identify our feelings, we can begin to decide what the consequential actions are. This **study of ourselves** begins the journey into understanding the confluent nature of our growth. The emotional intelligence curriculum is a means to that end. We begin to teach our children to manage their behavior inside and outside the classroom.

What do we mean by emotional literacy? Why is it important?

Emotional literacy is defined as the ability to know words and concepts to negotiate emotions.

We have tons of emotions going through our body all the time. They travel the emotional highway from our head to our stomach and back. Some of them just keep on moving; others get caught in our heads, and we focus on them. These feelings are never just good or bad. It's what we <u>do</u> about them that can have either wonderful or disastrous consequences.

Our children have these same emotions. They are just as powerful and complicated as our own. They travel the same highway. Children feel them and focus on them just like we do. The problem can be when they don't have ways to express to grown-ups what those emotions are called. Another problem arises because the emotions may not be caused by the same things. Because adults tend to see children's problems as "childish" or simply not important, we often don't give credence to those feelings.

The old question about the chicken or the egg is related to the relationship between thought and emotion. Which comes first? Scientists are beginning to see that parts of the brain work at different speeds and relate to each other in different ways.

- Are you aware of all the emotions that you feel? Try keeping a list of all the emotions you feel for a week. Get a little notebook, and every time you feel something write it down - sad, angry, foreboding, anxious, contemptuous, etc. At the end of each day, look over your list.

- Do you detect patterns in the emotions that you feel?

    Talk about these words:

    When you _____, I feel _____, so I _____.

- Does music change the way you feel?

Cockerton (1997) proved that soothing music at test time improved test scores. Calming music can both increase learner satisfaction and lower anxiety (Blood & Ferris, 1993). In general, music can affect your mental state (Jensen, 2003).

We know that music augments emotional release, listening skills, motor development, and scaffolding (Hudspeth, 1986).

- Can you tell when your boss is in a bad mood? Do you or one of your co-workers seem to know when the right time to approach him or her is? Emotional literacy helps us to learn to feel comfortable with ourselves and others. It's the way we begin to negotiate our own feelings and those of the people around us. Children can learn to observe other people's body language too.

People who accurately perceive others' emotions are better able to handle changes and build stronger social networks (Salovey, Bedell, Detweiler, & Mayer, 1999).

Activities
- Feelings Bingo:
- Even a four-year-old can keep a feelings journal:
- Conflict resolution table:
- Class feelings book:

You're Amazing! A Lesson in Emotional Literacy

The road to self efficacy begins with emotional literacy. Teachers and parents help children reach emotional literacy by teaching ways to identify and label emotions. We can:

- Provide environments in which children feel safe to share their feelings.

- Introduce a variety of feelings words, beginning with the primary emotions (happy, sad, mad, scared, surprised and disgusted) and gradually add words to expand children's feelings vocabulary (disappointed, excited, frustrated, worried, or jealous). In Appendix A, you'll find an exhaustive list of feelings.

- Teach feelings words by naming and discussing the emotions as children experience them. Observe facial expressions, tone of voice, and body language to assess their feelings.

- Make observational statements, such as "You look angry. What happened to make you feel that way?" In this way children have a name for their feeling and can then tell you about their situation.

- Class meetings provide an outlet for conflict resolution and discussions about feelings.

- Read and discuss emotion-related books. (*The Gunniwolf, The Owl & the Pussycat, A Fish Tale* are some of Dr. Rhythm's books.) Stop occasionally and ask children to identify the characters' feelings in the context of the story.

- Display photos and posters of people with various emotional expressions throughout the classroom or the house.

- Respect cultural variations in emotional expression.
- Watch yourself in a mirror or on video and see if you can observe changes in your own face and body as your emotions change.

Feelings Faces Class Meeting

Objective: To help children identify the range of emotions possible in a given situation and appreciate that not everyone feels the same way at the same time.

Materials: Enough paper plates stapled to a paint mixing stick or tongue depressor for each child to have two plates.

Preparation: Draw facial expressions on the plates on round sheets of paper and laminate them. Glue them to the plates and glue the plates to the sticks.

Procedure: Pass out the feelings face sticks to the children so that each child has two faces. With the help of the children, identify each feelings face. Make up short scenarios that are typical of children's experiences. At the end of the story, ask the children to show how that person might be feeling. The child who has that feeling should show his face stick by raising it in the air.

Sample story: Derek took the book away from Shaneka while she was reading it. Help the children notice that not everyone has the same opinion as to how the children in these stories will feel. For example, Emily might think that Shaneka will be angry, while others might think she would feel frustrated or sad.

Mood Wheel

Objective: To promote children's ability to identify and take ownership of their feelings.

Materials: This game is used with five or six children. Tag board cut into a circle. Have one for each child.

Preparation: Draw lines to divide the circle into fourths or as many divisions as you wish to make. On each section of the circle, draw a face that reflects one emotion (happy, sad, angry, afraid, etc). Write the emotion word next to the picture. Laminate. Put an arrow in the center of the wheel with a fastener, so that the arrow can be moved to point to any emotion on the wheel.

Procedure: Show one mood wheel to the children. Identify each emotion drawing. The leader begins the activity by moving her arrow to point to a feeling. She names the emotions, and then states a reason or event that might lead to someone feeling that way. "I get angry when I can't find my glasses." Describe the situations familiar to the children. Pass out a mood wheel to each child. One at a time, give the children a chance to indicate how they are feeling by turning their arrow to a certain feeling. Ask the children what leads to that feeling.

Variation: Make a mood wheel for all the children. Let them keep it at their desk or in their cubby to use to communicate their feelings to others. Use it when children are asked to write about their feelings on a daily basis.

One more thought: I talked for years to my own daughter, who was our youngest child with three male siblings, about feelings. I worked with her on the topic of owning her feelings. Alfred Adler said that we choose our behavior in response to our feelings. My daughter would often exclaim, "He made me mad!" I would explain to her that she chose to be mad, because her brother did something to her. She could choose to be mad, and then deal with the feeling. How she behaved as a result of that feeling was also her choice. How we respond behaviorally to our feelings will be a topic of a later lesson.

Feelings Bingo

Purpose: To associate feelings words with pictures.

Materials: Copy and print a sheet at the beginning of Part II for each student. Save one copy to cut up and choose from. Have enough buttons or tabs for each child to cover pictures.

Procedure: Play bingo!

Role plays

Do simple role-plays by asking children to Show how their body and face would look if:

- You got a birthday present
- A big dog barked at you.
- A friend put a worm in your hand.
- You found a snake on the playground.
- You fell down and tore your new clothes.
- A friend knocked down your blocks.

Recognizing Patterns in our Behavior?

- Look at our feelings journal. Which feelings appear more than others? Make a chart.

Fish's Feelings Chart (Sample)

Directions: Beforehand, you should write down all of your feelings for a week.

1. Pick the 10 feelings that you had the most during the week.
2. Write them on the first row of the chart.
3. Underneath each feeling, write the second and third most prevalent feelings.

	1	2	3	4	5	6	7	8	9	10	
1											
2											
3											

Now, what do we do about it?

> **"Choose Yourself" Overview**
>
> **Choose Yourself**
>
> Apply Consequential Thinking
> - Costs and benefits; Shift patterns.
>
> Navigate Emotions
> - Delay gratification; Choose emotions.
>
> Engage Intrinsic Motivation
> - Build internal drivers
>
> Shift to Optimism
> - Reframe thinking; Accept power and responsibility

Children are now ready to choose how they are going to respond. They will take responsibility for their own learning and behavior because they know they are in control. "Maybe I shouldn't just take that toy away from my sister."

Applying Consequential Thinking

- **How's that behavior been working for you?**

When I _____, _____ happens.

For grown-ups, as well as children, knowing how we react in learning situations--learning styles--is an important tool to begin an appreciation for life-long learning. Looking at patterns of behavior and the consequences of actions comprises the next goal. This phase is called **choosing yourself**. The children begin to learn about how their behavior affects others and how they learn best to complete the self-knowledge component.

Things for Adults to Think About

- A game that we play with college students is called "Pass the Pliers." We will all sit in a circle, in chairs or on the floor. I tell them that we are going to play an observation game. We are going to pass and receive the pliers either open or closed. The trick is to decide whether you have received them open or closed and then whether you're going to pass them either open or closed. The secret is that only people who have played the game before know when the pliers are open or closed. When we play the game, it is important to look at how we were feeling when we didn't now the rules, how we felt when we knew and others didn't, and how we felt afterward. Did we get mad? When did we feel like throwing in the towel?

Now imagine that you're a child, and the teacher is explaining long division to the class. Maybe you've just memorized your multiplication tables; no one has helped you to understand why the tables work. Other children in the class look like they understand exactly what the teacher is explaining. (You're comparing your inside to the other children's outside appearance. That's another issue for discussion.) Is that when you make the decision that you're just not good at math?

Teaching Children About Consequential Thinking. . .

If a child lives with criticism, he learns to condemn.

If a child lives with hostility, he learns to fight.

If a child lives with ridicule, he learns to be shy.

If a child lives with fear, he learns to be apprehensive.

If a child lives with shame, he learns to feel guilty.

If a child lives with tolerance, he learns to be patient.

If a child lives with encouragement, he learns to be confident.

If a child lives with acceptance, he learns to love.

If a child lives with approval, he learns to like himself.

If a child lives with recognition, he learns it is good to have a goal.

If a child lives with honesty, he learns what truth is.

If a child lives with fairness, he learns justice.

If a child lives with security, he learns to have faith in himself and those about him.

If a child lives with friendliness, he learns the world is a nice place in which to live, to love and be loved. Driekurs, R. 1972 pp. 28-29.

- Working with children in the area of consequential thinking can be a challenging affair. Natural/logical consequences are important to help young people mature and understand what behaviors create negative consequences, but parents and teachers need to be highly creative.

- We can argue about the pros and cons of being democratic when dealing with youngsters, but there is no denying that we can and do often manipulate their emotional states. Teachers can watch the looks on their students' faces when they say, "Put away everything on your desk. We're having a pop test."

    > There is a story of a child who fell of his chair in the classroom and everyone laughed. He enjoyed the attention, so he kept on doing it. The teacher quietly walked over to his table and removed the chair telling the child that he would need to stand up for the rest of the day since he had so much trouble sitting. Situation solved. The consequence was directly related to the action.

- In Dr. Rhythm's story, "A Fish Tale," we hear about a poor fisherman's wife named Gertrude who was greedy. Her husband, Herman, was given three wishes by a magic fish. She wanted a castle, to be queen of her island with maids, butlers, and all the food she could eat, but she wanted more. In the end, she lost everything. Now that's consequences!

From this. . .   to this. . .   and   back to this.

Navigate Emotions: What does that mean?
Deciding how to react to your feelings...

- *Delay gratification*
    Grandma was right! Count to 10.

- *Choose emotions on which to focus.*

A little brain talk about navigating emotions (changing the way we deal with our emotions).

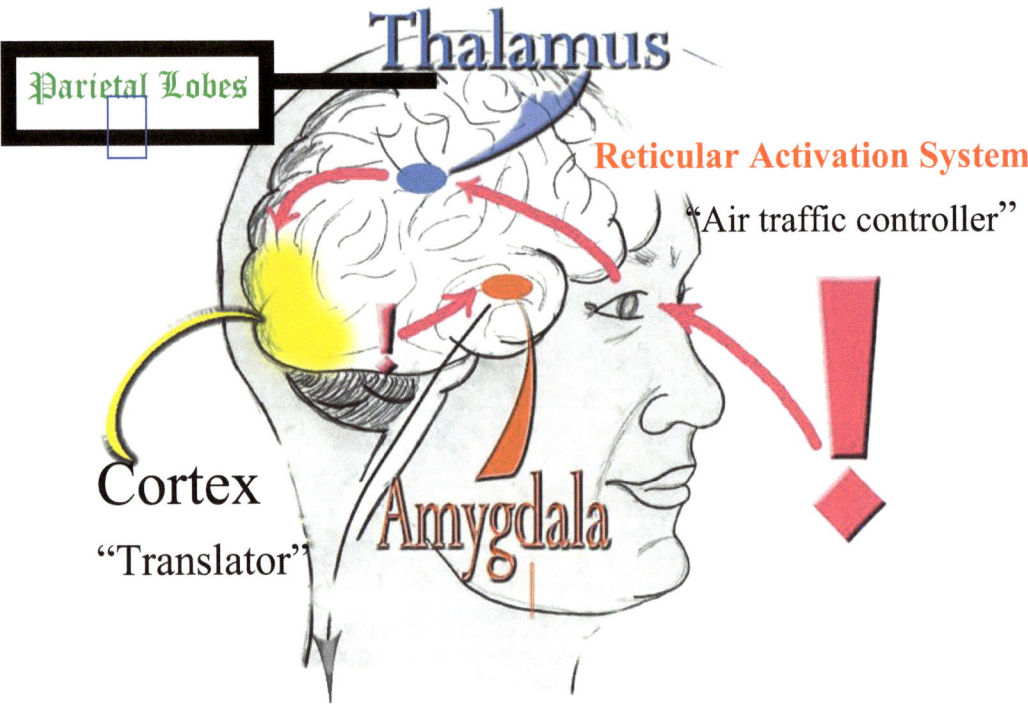

All sensory information comes through the amygdala (the two almond shaped points on the side of your head) into the limbic system. Stuff goes really fast in there.

The limbic system handles memory, emotion, kinesthetic information, and other stuff that our senses bring us. You can either act on that information - like if you touch a hot stove, you move your hand - or move it to the parietal lobes where you can evaluate the information.

Memory usually goes to the hippocampus for storage. Kinesthetic information can be handled in several different ways. Emotions can also be handled in several ways. If you see a big, hungry bear in the woods or a six-foot muscle man getting ready to slam you with a chair, your limbic system should take over in the "fight or flight" mode. If you feel threatened, you react quickly with words or actions. That's what happens when a toddler takes a toy from another toddler; they feel threatened. Another example is when you just finished paying your bills and realized that your account is at $10.00. Then, your wife comes in and tells you that she just ran through the garage door because she forgot to open it. Your "manhood" may feel threatened. Do you lash out or do you approach it logically?

It takes about six seconds for your "Reticular Activation System" to take over and carry those emotions that you feel to the parietal lobes where you can evaluate your actions. After you've punched holes in a few of your walls, you might want to try some EQ tricks. One of the oldest is to "count to ten" as grandma used to say. There are some others that children and grown-ups can use. We'll teach you those others in EQ training.

> Can you take the time
> To breathe
> When you feel like
> You're going
> To
> ## Explode?

Let's Talk About Intrinsic Motivation

Important Characteristics to Develop for Emotional Intelligence

Why is motivation important?

Things for adults to think about. . .

What's the difference between motivation and perseverance?

- Are you motivated by how you feel or by what you think (to the extent that these are separate)? How about compared to how others think and/or feel?

- Sometimes people say others "are not living up to their potential." What does that mean?

- Are you motivated by the same factors that motivate your friends?

- Which takes more motivation - to be a workaholic or for a workaholic to take a break?

- Dr. Rhythm's song, "So Many Ways to be Smart," is about using the multiple intelligences to look at the ways that we are smart. Parents and teachers can find the ways that their children are smart to motivate them to get better at what they're good at as well as using what the children are interested in to introduce them to new skills.

> **The Itsy Bitsy Spider went up the water spout**
> **Down came the rain and washed the spider out**
> **Out came the sun and dried up all the rain**
> **And the Itsy Bitsy Spider went up the spout again**

Perseverance and Young Children

There are many kinds of motivation. Extrinsic motivations come from desire for recognition or reward. Intrinsic motivation comes from a sense of purpose. Dr. Rhythm tells us at the beginning of the "Itsy Bitsy Spider" that it's about "perseverance." So in addition to the obvious studies about spiders and other arachnids, the gross and fine motor skills used in the song and dance (the spider stride), and the spatial relations arena of up and down; we have the emotional intelligence paradigm – selecting goals for ourselves. (The emotional intelligence paradigm consists of **learning words to negotiate feelings, learning to accept your feelings and choose actions appropriately, and selecting noble goals for yourself.**) Here we find the character trait of perseverance. It's not a big jump to see the connection between motivation and perseverance. People who persevere know that their actions will make a difference. They feel that they have control.

Some will say that, theoretically speaking, young children only focus on the concrete aspects of concepts and the visible aspects of experience, not the abstract meanings or internal, less visible features or motivations. Our job as teachers and parents is to help them make the transition to being able to imagine what cannot be seen and to think abstractly. So the grownup introduces the concept of perseverance by asking, "Have you ever tried and tried to do something?" The ensuing discussion should be enlightening for the children and the adults. The key is to learn as much as you can about the child's point of view that has contributed to his or her own unique meanings to the word perseverance.

Another theoretical consideration involves young children's inability to make logical connections between causes and effects. The song, "The Itsy Bitsy Spider," certainly helps in that area. The rain washes the spider down the spout and the heat from the sun dries up the rainwater (evaporation). We can help children make the transition toward understanding logical causal connections between events through science experiments using a hose, a tube, and a plastic spider. Put the spider in the tube and flush it with water. Have the children make predictions about what they think will happen.

Some people will tell you that young children don't make hypotheses, but we can certainly help them make the transitions to the concrete and formal operations stages by providing experiences in critical thinking.

Children's ideas change and grow gradually. Rarely does thinking change dramatically. It goes through slow transitions from less to more mature thinking in all domains. Change occurs as children have many opportunities to try out their ideas, see how they work, and then modify them based on what happened. It also occurs as they have new experiences that give them new content to use in trying out and building new ideas.

Quotes about Motivation and Perseverance

People become MOTIVATED when you guide them to the source of their own power.
                                                                Anita Roddick

People can be divided into three groups:
   Those who make things happen
   Those who watch things happen, and
   Those who wonder what happened.

Woody Allen

Whatever you can do, or dream you can do, begin it. Boldness has genius, power, and magic in it.

Goethe

Work hard and give it your best shot, never be a quitter. Each day do a little better than the day before because no matter how good you are, you should always try to be better.

Charley Taylor, NFL Wide Receiver

Put perseverance into action:

- Do something today that you promised to do yesterday.

- Work a little harder or a few minutes longer on a duty or assignment that is difficult for you.

- Choose a job that you've been putting off, decide to persevere until the job is finished, and then DO IT.

- List three tasks you recently completed, and list the reasons you finished them. Why were you motivated? Could you use those motivations on a different task?

- Recognize a friend, teacher, or family member who has persevered to finish a difficult task. Tell them. Write them a note.

- List all of your actions and activities from the last 24 hours, and sort them into "what I chose" and "what others chose for me."

- When a child comes to you with a problem, don't fix it. Instead, support him and help him understand the problem. Offer encouragement to generate original solution(s).

In The Harvard Business Review, the headlining breakthrough idea (out of ten) for 2010 is that what motivates "knowledge workers" the most is not recognition, incentives, interpersonal support, or clear goals. It's a sense of progress. "On days when workers have the sense they're making headway in their jobs, or when they receive support that helps them overcome obstacles," the authors write, "their emotions are most positive and their drive to succeed is at its peak." On the other hand, days when they spin their wheels or encounter roadblocks to meaningful accomplishment, their moods and motivation are lowest. The article is based on a multiyear study that tracked day-to-day activities, emotions, and motivation levels of hundreds of knowledge workers in a wide range of settings. So what advice does The Business Review offer to those in charge? "Scrupulously avoid impeding progress by changing goals autocratically, being indecisive, or holding up resources. Negative events generally have a greater effect on people's emotions, perceptions, and motivation than positive ones, and nothing is more demotivating than a setback -- the most prominent type of event on knowledge workers' worst days."

Did being washed out of the water spout stop the Itsy Bitsy Spider?

NO! He went right back up again.

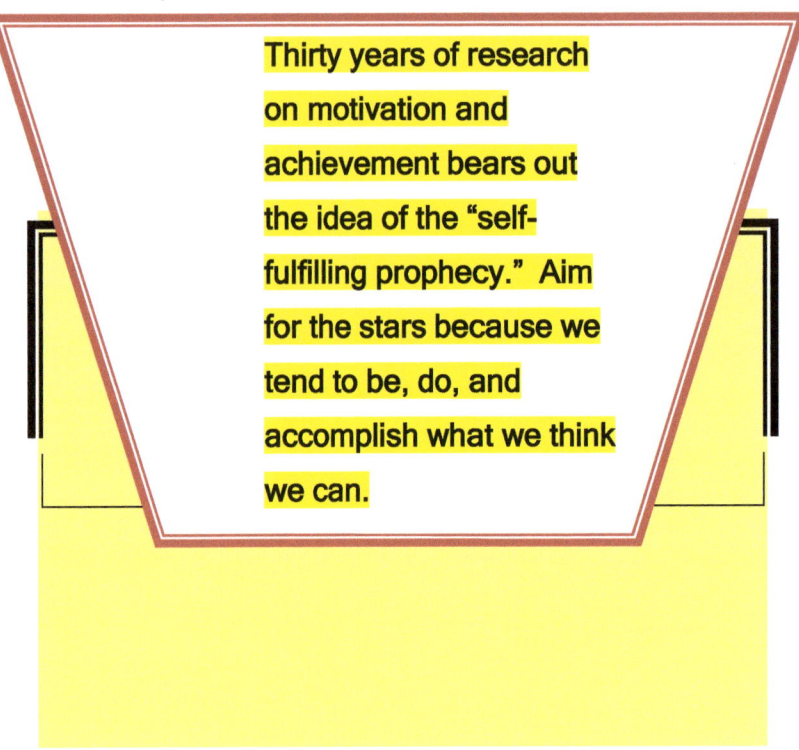

Thirty years of research on motivation and achievement bears out the idea of the "self-fulfilling prophecy." Aim for the stars because we tend to be, do, and accomplish what we think we can.

Optimism: Realizing your own power.

Why Is Optimism Important?

Optimism is the realization that you have power over your destiny.

hope - the general feeling that some desire will be fulfilled; "in spite of his troubles he never gave up hope"

sanguineness, sanguinity - feeling sanguine; optimistically cheerful and confident.

Things for Adults to Think About

Having a positive mental attitude is asking how something can be done rather than saying it can't be done Bo Bennett

Thomas Alva Edison was known for his positive attitude towards life. One story goes like this:

> Edison was in the process of inventing his well known invention, the incandescent lamp. The headache in this process was to find a suitable material that glows on heating. He was trying a lot of combinations to suit his need but in vain (it is a shame that tungsten was not popular in those days). Our man was not going to give up, but his assistant was not as optimistic as Edison. One day he asked Edison, with total loss of hope, what on earth he was trying to do and how did he intend to find the right substance in this way. Edison replied "By checking these hundreds of compounds, I have eliminated the substances that do not glow. So I would soon be able to find the right substance in this way."

> It is said is that an optimistic person will be happy with a glass that it is half filled with water and a pessimistic person will be disappointed that it is half empty. Optimism is the only way of converting failure to success.

> Can you think of a problem that you tried to solve through trial and error? Did you want to give up? Was there something that kept you going?

> If you will call your troubles experiences, and remember that every experience develops some latent force within you, you will grow vigorous and happy, however

adverse your circumstances may seem to be. John Heywood (English Playwright and Poet, 1497-1580)

What was your last struggle? Did it leave you with a sense of being proud? Pride is associated with struggle. What comes easy for us, we take for granted, but when we have to struggle to obtain results, whether successful or not, we can come away with more knowledge than we had before.

If you realized how powerful your thoughts are, you would never think a negative thought. Peace Pilgrim (American Teacher and Spiritual leader and Peace Prophet, 1908-1981)

What seems to us as bitter trials are often blessings in disguise. Oscar Wilde (Irish Poet, Novelist, Dramatist and Critic, 1854-1900)

A pessimist sees the difficulty in every opportunity; an optimist sees the opportunity in every difficulty. Winston Churchill (1874-1965)

Positive things happen to positive people. Sarah Beeny - (1971-)

I found that in prison that I had more time to read the Bible, I had more time to contemplate life, and more time to look upon my fellow man And I worked very hard during the period in there to help other people in the same situation And I think that even in the most dastardly people, there is a goodness there, and you've got to find that goodness.
Alan Bond -

The act of helping people helps with optimism because you can see the positive effects of doing something to improve the world

I've always worked very, very hard, and the harder I worked, the luckier I got. Alan Bond (1938 -)

Are some people just lucky? Do you consider yourself lucky? Is there something called "dumb luck"?

optimism - the feeling that all is going to turn out well, a tendency to expect the best possible outcome or dwell on the most hopeful aspects of a situation. The doctrine that states this world is the best of all possible worlds. The belief that the universe is improving and that good will ultimately triumph over evil.

Talking with Children About Optimism

Read good books, smile more, spend time with optimistic people, do good deeds for those around you, listen to good news (there is plenty!), and bring good news to others.

- Model optimism in your daily routine. Express your appreciation for things that you often take for granted - beautiful trees, people helping other people, or just time spent together with friends.

- Learn to laugh at yourself. Humor can get us through the tough times and the rough times. Let children see you laugh at yourself when you get your words mixed up or get mixed up on a daily schedule.

Things to Do with Children

- Provide opportunities for problem-solving and making choices. Encourage children to choose which learning centers they want to work in, which activities they want to do, which colors they want to paint with. When problems occur, such as juice spills or balls going into a water puddle, invite the children to think of solutions.

- In Dr. Rhythm's story, "The Apple Tree and her Blessings," the small tree wants to be special by having stars on her branches like the tall oak trees all around her, but she learns that she's been special all along.

Develop children's language skills, and weave the following vocabulary words into your day:

confidence
hopefulness
cheerfulness
pride
happy
gratified

content
challenge
appreciation
funny
humor
nonsense

People who learn optimism skills are more motivated, more successful, have higher levels of achievement, plus significantly better physical and mental health (Seligman, 1991).

Circumstances and Optimism

<u>Circumstances can create unfairness.</u>
- Let's say you interview for a job, and another applicant who is less qualified but "connected" gets the job.
- People often make judgments based on their biases and prejudices. The guilt or innocence of a person suspected of committing a crime is often decided before the trial begins. Many of us form opinions about the mental, moral, and physical abilities of others based solely on their race, gender, ethnicity, or lifestyle. **Is that fair?**
- *Fairness* is a controversial, even volatile, subject. It's not uncommon to have groups feel that they are being discriminated against in a society with people from many cultures and backgrounds living together. That cry of discrimination comes from the **fear** of being treated unfairly.

Ask yourself:
 1. Have you ever been in a situation where you felt that others judged you without

Finding the sunshine in the rain

knowing you?
2. Have you ever been treated unfairly? How did you feel? How did you react?
3. Do you think people should turn their heads if following the rules means losing?
4. Were there ever situations and circumstances in your life that have resulted in unfairness?
5. Have you ever made a decision or acted in a way that wasn't based on applying rules equitably?

Growing up in poverty situations is certainly a circumstance that would be considered unfair. Children can't help where, when, or into what family they're born. Over 25% of our children are born into poverty households. Encouraging optimism would certainly help children overcome their circumstances. Some situations are just not fair, but the children's view of their situation can be changed. Following are some examples of ways to overcome circumstances and create optimistic children:

- **Children are respected, nurtured, and challenged.** They enjoy close, warm relationships with adults and other children in their classroom. They frequently interact and communicate with peers and adults; they do not spend long periods of time waiting, being ignored, or isolated. Children enjoy and look forward to school.
- **Children participate in varied social situations.** They learn important social and self-regulatory skills through adult guidance. Not all children are expected to develop at the same rate; individual needs and abilities are accommodated in all activities. The children learn to make the best of their situation. They become more hopeful, resilient, and self confident.

- **Children are able to make meaningful decisions throughout the day.** They can choose from a variety of activities and decide what type of products they want to create, engage in important conversations with friends, and exercise their curiosity. As we remember from Chapter 3, choice is at the heart of becoming optimistic. Children learn to recover from poor choices through adult guidance and understanding as well as benefit from healthy choices.

Children can begin to develop a sense of justice. Begin by asking children the following questions:

1. What does fair mean?

2. Do you feel like you're treated fairly at home? How do you feel when someone treats you unfairly?
3. Is it okay to cheat to win a game? Why or why not? Would it be okay for someone else to cheat to beat you in a game?

You can also discuss these words to develop children's language skills.

fairness	honesty	cheating
dishonest	equitable	just
injustice	rules	unfair

Is courage important? Things for adults to think about. . .

- Fear is a basic emotion. Have you listened to the evening news lately? Ours is a violent society. Many of us have developed strategies for coping with fear.
- Do you think society exploits our fears because some people enjoy the adrenaline rush created by the need for excitement?
- As with all emotions, we all experience fear. The question is: How do we face it? It can either immobilize us or motivate us.
    Listen to Dr. Rhythm's story, The Gunniwolf. How does the little girl handle her fear?
- Fear is often the basis for many of our actions and reactions. Take envy, for example. Is it really the fear of not being good enough or having enough? What about anger? Is it generated by a fear of loss? If we can trace our anger, jealous, or greedy feelings to this fear, how important is it to summon the courage to overcome fear?

Should we protect our children from fear?

There is a strong emphasis in the newest learning standards for early childhood and primary grade children to teach the difference between "reality" and "fantasy." This practice appears to be perpetuated by a lack of understanding of how children grow and develop. Theorists tell us that reality, according to children in the preoperational stage (before age 7), is based on their experience. What is real to a young child may be fantasy to an adult.

The converse is also true. Have you ever tried to help a three year-old understand the concept of a stranger? Chances are you either got nowhere or you ended up making the child afraid of everyone. Very young children are simply not ready to generalize information from one situation to another.

Without question, we want our children to experience the innocence of childhood, but protecting them and shielding them from fear can be a disservice. When children experience child-sized fears, they gradually build strategies for coping with their fears. Childhood fears are a normal part of growing up.

So think of some of the things that frightened you when you were young. What strategies did you use to face your fears then? What fears do you have now? Do you use any coping strategies?

More questions to ask children. . .

- What is fear? Is it ever a good thing? Does it keep us safe sometimes? Can you think of a fear that turned out to be a good thing?
- Do you think grown-ups are ever afraid? Ask grown-ups around you to describe a time when they were afraid. What did they do?
- Think of a time when you were afraid. What were you afraid of? What did you do? Will you be afraid next time?
- Think of ways to stop being afraid or facing fear like whistling or drawing a picture of what made you afraid. How many things can you think of?

Developing language skills . . .
Weave these words into your day:

afraid	coping	brave
danger	challenge	fear
courage	imagination	strategy

Dr. Rhythm's story "The Legend of Bo Didley" is the tale of a courageous young boy who conquered fear, had the motivation and perseverance to learn to play the drums, and ended up saving his village through his courage, his music, and some creative thinking.

Thinking about creativity... *Is it important?*

Robert Sternberg (2006) says that creative people routinely approach problems in novel ways. Creative people habitually:

- Look for ways to see problems that other people don't look for;
- take risks that other people are afraid to take;
- have the courage to defy the crowd and to stand up for their own beliefs;
- believe in their own ability to be creative;
- seek to overcome obstacles and challenges to their views that other people give in to; and
- are willing to work hard to achieve creative solutions.

So, why is creativity even important? It is important because the world is changing at a far greater pace than it ever has before, and people need constantly to cope with new and unusual kinds of tasks and situations. Learning in this era must be lifelong, and people constantly need to be thinking in new ways. The problems we confront, whether in our families, communities, or nations, are novel and difficult, and we need to think creatively and divergently to solve these problems. The technologies, social customs, and tools available to us in our lives are replaced almost as quickly as they are introduced. We need to think creatively to thrive, and, at times, even to survive.

Daniel Pink, author of *A Whole New Mind: Moving from the Information Age to the Conceptual Age*, writes that the future belongs to a different kind of person with a different kind of mind. He notes, "The era of "left-brain" dominance and the Information Age it engendered is giving way to a new world in which artistic and holistic "right-brain" abilities mark the fault line between who gets ahead and who falls behind."

Creativity and innovation come with exposure, practice and personal growth. Our culture of standardized testing ignores the cultivation of these skill sets and aptitudes in an entire generation of children. We know that kids love popular culture; so let's teach them how to "read" it, critique it, know when it is good and when it is bad. That kind of literacy leads to important jobs in the creative-services sector and other kinds of research, entrepreneurship and invention.

Talking with children about creativity

- Play "what if?" Make up situations and problems for children to think about and respond to. For example, "What did they do before TV?" or "What if we didn't have soap?" or "How would the world be different if we didn't have the color blue?"
- Teachers can ask children what things are used for. They can show that things have different uses through art. For example, we use straws for drinking or blowing paint or stringing or gluing. Another example is clothes pins. They can be used to hold sponges, close a chip bag, and make an animal . . . what else? Encourage children to use materials in different ways.

    Simple things like pencils have so many shapes, sizes, and uses – drawing pencils, drafting pencils, fat pencils, skinny pencils, colored pencils, eye pencils, etc. What can you do with them? How do changes in design make pencils more useful?

- Offering choices in the classroom and at home allows children to make good and bad choices and learn the rewards or consequences. Children can learn to weigh out pros and cons of different options.
- Involve children in decision-making activities. Perhaps we only have $25.00 to spend on doing something fun. Do we want to go to the movies or have pizza?
- Let your children solve their own problems. Consistently bailing them out encourages dependency and prohibits practicing "creative solutioning."

Develop children's language skills and continue to discuss creativity and resourcefulness by weaving the following vocabulary words into your day.

creativity	critique
imagination	ingenuity
opportunity	curiosity
invention	appreciation
problems	resources
solutions	resourcefulness

> **"Give Yourself" Overview**
>
> **Give Yourself**
>
> **Increase Empathy**
> - Expand feelings beyond self
>
> **Act on Noble Goals**
> - Engage in lifelong vision

Since we look at the whole child, we want to help our children become good citizens. We focus on building strong values, building learning communities, helping others.

Give Yourself

For grown-ups and children, the "give yourself" component also involves goals. It involves empathy—the ability to expand feelings beyond ourselves and goals. We can act on noble goals and engage in a lifelong vision or work toward a simple short term goal.

Josh Freedman tells us that Noble Goals really means putting purpose into everyday action. If your purpose is supporting equity, how can you build more equity between the people in the elevator today? If your purpose is sustaining a vibrant earth, how can you change what you buy for lunch to be more sustainable? If your purpose is nurturing compassion, how can you think and feel as you wash the dishes so you end that experience more compassionate?

In other words: Consider the alignment between WHAT you are doing each moment, each day -- HOW you are doing that, and WHY? Is your intention coming through both in the action and in the way that action is undertaken?

Empathy

Empathy gives us the power to reach beyond our own experiences by feeling what other people experience. Daniel Goleman writes that empathy leads to caring, altruism, and compassion. Seeing things from another's perspective breaks down biased stereotypes, thus bringing tolerance and acceptance of diversity.

Give Yourself | Empathy

Empathy means feeling in parallel to someone else's feeling.

What behaviors does empathy create?

What behaviors does empathy create?
Team players, cooperative learners, communal consciousness . . .

In a cabin in a wood
Little man by his window stood
Saw a rabbit hopping by
Knocking at his door.

"Help me! Help me! Help me!" he said
"I need a place to rest my head."
"Little rabbit, come inside
Safely to abide."

Why are empathy and compassion important things to think about?

- *Compassion and empathy begin to develop during early infancy. Many neuroscientists assume that we are "biologically wired" for these emotions; but adults would do well to recognize and nurture this natural inclination toward caring.*

    Have your children ever seen you cry? What happened? Do you agree that young children are naturally compassionate? How can we help children develop ways of displaying compassion and empathy?

- *Compassion and empathy encompass respect for all living things, even the tiniest of creatures that have no voice to speak for themselves.*

    Have you ever stepped on an ant? How is that different from pulling a dog's tail? How is pulling a dog's tail different from hitting someone?

We have found research that supports the idea that people benefit health-wise from helping others:

- A Boston College study found that patients with chronic pain fared better when they counseled other patients who were also in pain. They felt less depression, less disability, and their intense pain was reduced.
- The Buck Institute for Age Research in California found a connection between volunteerism and longevity among older people. Elderly participants who did volunteer work for more than four hours a week were less likely to die during the study period.
- A Miami study of patents with HIV found that those who demonstrated strong altruistic characteristics had lower levels of stress hormones.
- A study of 150 heart patients found that those who talked about themselves at length and used more first-person pronouns did worse on treadmill tests than those who referred to themselves less.

75

Empathy

is the way

we treat all there is in life

- ourselves,

our bodies,

our imaginations and dreams,

our neighbors, our enemies,

our air, our water,

our earth, our animals,

our death, our space,

and our time.

Compassion is a spirituality

as if creation mattered.

It is treating all creation

as holy and as divine...

Talking with Children about Compassion and Empathy

- What does it mean to be a friend?
- What does it mean to be kind to animals?

    Think about a time when someone hurt you? How did you feel?

- Read the "Little Rabbit" poem on page 74. Teach it to your children. (You could make up hand motions to go with it.)

    Ask the children to describe how the rabbit feels.

    Why is he tired?

    Did something frighten him? Has he been running from a fox?

    Does the man seem to understand how the little rabbit feels? He wants to help him. Discuss the man's kindness.

- Ask the children to think of a time when they were hurt or sick.

    Who took care of them?

    How did that person take care of them?

    Ask them if they have ever helped take care of someone who was sick or hurt.

    Have they helped someone feel better?

    How did it feel?

Develop children's language skills and continue your discussion of compassion and empathy by weaving the following vocabulary words into your day:

caring	helping	feelings
compassion	kindness	abide
empathy	thoughts	

- Point out ways children show compassion:

  "Joesphine, I see you are helping Ernie pick up the pieces of his puzzle that fell on the ground." Be careful to **validate** rather than reward.

- Expand children's ideas of ways to help those in need. For example, one set of teachers discussed a child's idea to gather food for an animal shelter, and the school as a whole adopted the project.

- Plan ways to engage children in acts of compassion. Sample projects include bringing in clothes for children who are homeless or abused, serving meals at a homeless shelter, or conducting a winter coat exchange. One group of children adopted the elderly in a nearby retirement home and sent letters and pictures to cheer them. One teacher talked about sending prayers on the wind to children in need around the world.

The process we use to understand another person's feelings and model an empathetic response is an important part of emotional literacy. Teaching children to identify the feelings of another person will lead to emotional intelligence and a positive self-concept.

- Demonstrate pleasure in another person's relief or comfort by sharing happiness. Sometimes children will be jealous of another child who receives a birthday present. You can use the activities above and ask the children how they would help another child who was in that situation.
- Identify the distress of another person. (James is crying - he looks sad)

    Figure out what is happening. (Let's ask him why he is sad)

    Decide how others might feel in the same situation. (He fell down on the playground. I cry too when I hurt myself.)

- Assess the needs of the other person and try to help them. (I'll get him a wet cloth and some water.)
- When reading a storybook talk about what the characters are feeling.
- Set aside a half-hour to really **listen** to someone.
- Experiment with body language. Since empathy is critical to communication, much of the message is in tone or body language.
    - Try saying the same word in many different ways.
    - Play "feelings charades." Have one person act out a feeling and others try to guess what it is.
    - Make a set of feeling flashcards with faces showing different emotions. Discuss what blend of emotions is apparent in each.
- Visit a hospital or go to the Special Olympics in your area. (www.specialolympics.org)
- When you receive a gift, think of something you have that you could give away.
- Find one of your most prized possessions to give to someone who needs it more than you do.
- Next time you have a disagreement with someone, let him or her know that even though you disagree, you understand and respect the way they feel.

"For compassion to be effective and healthy it needs to be disciplined and focused. It requires discretion both to whom you express compassion, and in the measure of the compassion itself. It is recognizing when compassion should be expressed and when it should be withheld or limited. Discipline in compassion is knowing that being truly compassionate sometimes requires withholding compassion. Because compassion is not an expression of the bestower's needs but a response to the recipient's needs. Am I more compassionate with strangers than with close ones? If yes, why? Is the compassion coming from guilt? Does my compassion for others compromise my own needs? Am I helping others at the expense of helping myself? Perhaps the contrary is the case: Does my compassion for my family and close ones overshadow others needs? Is my compassion impulsive and careless? Do I assess the measure of compassion necessary for a given situation? Is it commensurate with the recipient's needs? Can I possibly be hurting him with my compassion? Does my compassion overwhelm others? Is it respectful? Do I give too much or too little? Do others take advantage of my compassionate nature? When I see a needy person do I impetuously express compassion out of guilt or pity without any discretion? Do I commit the "crime" of compassion by helping him with something harmful (give him money to buy a harmful substance etc.)? Do I apply myself to determine this person's needs and help him in the best way possible?

For compassion to be fully realized, it needs bonding. It requires creating a channel between giver and receiver - mutuality that extends beyond the moment of need. A bond that continues to live on is the most gratifying result of true compassion. Do you bond with the one you have compassion for, or do you remain apart? Does your interaction achieve anything beyond a single act of sympathy?"

By Simon Jacobson - From A Spiritual Guide to the Omer by Simon Jacobson - Reprinted with the permission.

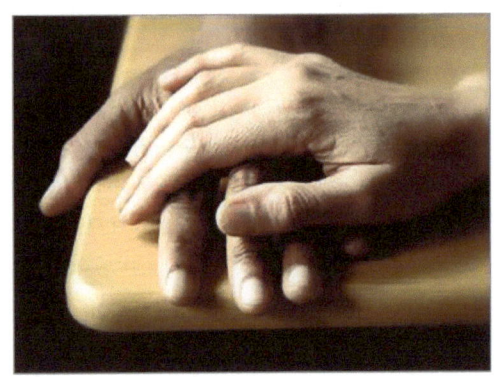

Goals

	Noble Goals Support Values
Give Yourself	Universal Values honesty respect responsibility fairness (justice) compassion (love) Institute for Global Ethics www.globalethics.org

Let's get rid of these   **And get these**

Low EQ   **High EQ**

Blaming	Bouncing back
Unforgiving	Listening
Defending	Empathizing
Stonewalling	Risking
Judging	Flexing

REFERENCES

Arsenio, W.F., Cooperman, S., & Lover, A. (2000). "Affective predictors of preschoolers' aggression and acceptance: Direct and indirect effects." *Developmental Psychology*, 36 (4), 438-448.

Bar-On, R. (2007). "How Important Is It to Educate People to Be Emotionally Intelligent, and Can It Be Done?" *Educating People to Be Emotionally Intelligent*, Praeger, (1) 10.

Barr, R. D. & Parrett, W.H. (2001). *Hope fulfilled for at-risk and violent youth: K-12 programs that work.* Needham Heights, MA: Allyn & Bacon.

Barton, P. & Coley R. (2007). "The Family: America's Smallest School." A policy report. Princeton, NJ: Educational Testing Service.

Beaty, J. (2008). Skills for preschool teachers. Upper Saddle River, NJ: Pearson Education, Inc.

Beck, I., McKeown, M.G., & Kucan, L. (2002). *Bringing words to life.* New York, NY: Guilford Press.

Blood, D.J. & Ferriss, S.J. (1993, February). Effects of background music on anxiety, satisfaction with communication, and productivity. *Psychological Reports,* 72(1), 171-7.

Bluestein, J. (2001). *Creating emotionally safe schools: A guide for educators and parents.* Deerfield Beach, FL: Health Communications, Inc.

Boyer, E. (2004) in Murfee, E. *Eloquent evidence: Arts at the core of learning.* Washington, DC: National Assembly of State Arts Agencies.

Brackett, M.A., Mayer, J.D., Warner, R.M. (2004). Emotional Intelligence and its relation to everyday behaviour. Personality and Individual Differences, 36 (6), 1387-1402.

Bray, D. W. (1976). The Assessment Center Method. In R.L. Craig (Ed.), *Training and Development Handbook* . New York: McGraw-Hill.

Bredekamp, S. & Copple, C., (Eds.). (1997). *Developmentally appropriate practice in early childhood programs.* Washington, DC: National Association for the Education of Young Children.

Caine, R. N. & Caine, G. (1994). *Making connections: Teaching and the Human Brain.* Menlo Park, CA: Addison-Wesley Publishing Co.

Caine, R. N. & Caine, G. (1997). *Education on the edge of possibility.* Alexandria, VA: Association for Supervision and Curriculum Development.

Cherniss, C., Extein, M., Goleman, D., Weissberg, R.P. (2006). "Emotional intelligence: What does the research really indicate?" *Educational Psychologist*, 41(4), 239-245.

Cokerton, T., Moore, S., & Norman, D. (1997, December). Cognitive test Performance and background music. *Perceptual and Motor Skills,* 85, 1435-8.

Coles, R. (1997). *The moral intelligence of children.* New York: Penguin Group.

Committee for Children. (2002). *Second Step.* Seattle, WA: via Internet on June 4, 2002~http://www.cfchildren.org/evals.html.

Cooper, R. K. & Sawaf, A. (1998). *Executive EQ: Emotional intelligence in leadership and organizations.* East Rutherford, NJ: Berkley Publishing Group.

Davidson, R. J., & & Sutton, S. K. (1995). Affective neuroscience: The emergence of discipline. *Current Opinion in Neurobiology,* 5 (2), 217-224.

Damasio, & Lenzen,M. in Scientific American Mind: April, 2005. Retrieved from the Internet April 22, 2005 from http://www.scientificamerican.com/article.cfm?id=feeling-our-emotions

Dunn, L. & Kontos, S. (1997). What have we learned about developmentally appropriate practice? *Young Children,* 52(5), 4_13.

Durlak & Weissberg, R.P. (2005) as cited in Cherniss, C., Extein, M., Goleman, D., Weissberg, R.P. (2006). Emotional intelligence: What does the research really indicate? *Educational Psychologist,* 41 (4), 239-245.

Erikson, E. H. (1959). *Identity and the life cycle.* New York: International Universities Press, Inc.

Espinosa, L. (2010). Getting it Right for Young Children from Diverse Backgrounds. Boston: Pearson Learning Solutions.

Feist, G. J., & Barron, F. (1996, June). *Emotional intelligence and academic intelligence in career and life success.* Paper presented at the Annual Convention of the American Psychological Society, San Francisco, CA.

Fiedeldey-Van Dijk, C. & Jensen, A. (2007). *Six Seconds Emotional Intelligence Assessment Youth Version (SEI-YV) – Technical Manual,* Six Seconds (in press).

Fish, B. (2008). *Families Uniting Through Literature: A family emotional intelligence program.* Paper presented at the International Conference of the National Association for the Education of Young Children, Dallas, TX.

Fish, B., (2003). *Why teach emotional intelligence?* [Brochure]. Jackson, MS: FishyRhythms Publishing .

Fish, B. (2002). *An Examination of the Mississippi Superintendents' Level of Support for the Emotional Intelligence Curriculum.* Unpublished doctoral dissertation. Jackson State University. Jackson, Mississippi.

Fleishman, E., & Harris, E. F. (1962). Patterns of leadership behavior related to employee grievances and turnover. *Personnel Psychology,* 15, 43-56.

Freedman, J. M.. "A 2000-2001 Self-Science EQ Curriculum Pilot Study: Self-Science Pilot Initial Report. June 01, 2001" via Internet http://www.6seconds.org/eqtoday/pilotstudy.html.

Freedman, J. (2003). "Key Lessons from 35 Years of Social-Emotional Education: How Self-Science Builds Self-Awareness, Positive Relationships, and Healthy Decision-Making." *Perspectives in Education* 21(4):69-80.

Freedman, J, Ghini, M. & Jensen, A. (2005). *Six Seconds Emotional Intelligence Assessment (SEI).* San Francisco: Six Seconds.

Freedman, J., Ghini, M., & Fieldeldey-van Dijk, C. (2006). "White Paper: Emotional Intelligence and Performance," www.6seconds.org/sei.

Frost, J. L., Wortham, S. C., and Reifel, S. (2001). Play and Child Development. New Jersey: Upper Saddle River.

Gardner, H. (1983) *Frames of mind*. New York: Basic Books.

Gazzaniga, M. (1988). *Mind matters: How mind and brain interact to create our conscious lives.* Boston: Houghton-Mifflin/MIT Press.

Glasser, W. (1988). *Choice theory in the classroom*. New York, NY: HarperCollins Publishers, Inc.

Goffin, S. G. & Wilson, S. (2001). *Curriculum models and early childhood education: Appraising the relationship.* 2nd Ed. Upper Saddle River, NJ: Merrill Prentice Hall.

Goleman, D. (1995). *Emotional intelligence*. New York: Bantam Books.

Goleman, D. (1998). "Toward a model emotional literacy curriculum." via Internet ~ http://www.feel.org/articles/goleman.html.

Hart, B. & Risley, T. (2002). Meaningful differences in the everyday experience of young children. Boston: Brookes Publishing, Inc.

Hawkins, J. D., & Catalano, R. F. (1992). *Communities that Care*. San Francisco, CA.: Jossey_Bass, Inc.

Hawkins, J., Kosterman, R., Catalano, R., Hill, J., Abbott, R. (2008). Effects of Social Development Intervention in Childhood 15 Years Later. Archives of Pediatrics & Adolescent Medicine, 162(12): 1133-1141.

Heidemann, S. & Hewitt, D. (1992). *Pathways to play: Developing play skills in young children*. St. Paul, MN: Redleaf Press.

Hemphill, J. K. (1959). Job description for executives. *Harvard Business Review*, 37(5), 55-67.

Hernandez, D. J. (1995) "Changing demographics: Past and future demands for early childhood programs." in *Long-term outcomes of early childhood programs*. on line at http://futureofchildren.org/information2826/information_show.html.

Hoy, G. (1998). *Imagination and creativity in education*. Santa Monica, CA: Enchante Publishing.

Hudspeth, C. (1986). The cognitive and behavioral consequences of using music and poetry in a fourth grade language arts classroom. *The Reading Teacher*. 40(1), 77-80.

Hunter, J. E., & Hunter, R. F. (1984). Validity and utility of alternative predictors of job performance. *Psychological Bulletin*, 76(1), 72-93. 24

Izard, C. E. & Read, P. B. (1986). *Measuring emotions in infants and children.* Vol.2.Cambridge CB2 IRP: Cambridge University Press.

Jensen, A. & Freedman, J. (2006). *Assessment of School Climate*. San Francisco: Six Seconds. Regression analysis from Freedman, J. & Fieldeldey-van Dijk, C. "White Paper: School Climate and School Success," Six Seconds (in press).

Jensen, E. (1998). *Teaching with the brain in mind*. Alexandria, VA: Association for Supervision and Curriculum Development.

Jensen, E. (2003). *Tools for engagement*. San Diego, CA: The Brain Store, Inc. Kagan's study (as cited in Kotulak, 1997)

Kaufman, P., Alt, M.N., Chapman, C.D. (2001). "Dropout rates in the United States, 2000." *Statistical Analysis Report*. MPR, Berkeley: CA.

Kohn, A. (1990). *The Brighter Side of Human Nature*. New York, New York: Basic Books

Kohn, A. (1999). *The Schools Our Children Deserve: Moving Beyond Traditional Classrooms and "Tougher Standards"*. Portsmouth, NH: Heinemann.

Kolb, G.R. (1996). Read with a beat: Developing literacy through music and song. *The Reading Teacher*. 50(1), 76-77.

Kostelnik, M., Whiren, A., Soderman, A., Stein, L., & Gregory, K. (2000). Guiding young children's social development. Albany, NY: Delmar.

Kostelnik, M., Whiren, A., & Soderman, A. (2010). Developmentally appropriate curriculum. Upper Saddle River, NJ: Pearson Education, Inc.

Kotulak, R. (1996). *Inside the brain*. Kansas City, MO: Andrews and McMeel.

Ledoux, J. (1996). *The emotional brain*. New York, NY: Simon and Schuster.

Lohman (2003) in Nyborg, H. (ed.) The scientific study of general intelligence. Boston, MA: Pergamon.

McNamara, S. (2006) "Emotional Intelligence, The Generation Game: Learn the Rules so children will too!" Unpublished Masters Thesis.

Marquis, J. (October 17, 1996). A real brainteaser. *Los Angeles Times*, p. B-2.

Maslow (1943) Self actualization interviews. New York, NY: Academic Press

Maslow (1969) Toward a psychology of being. New York, NY: Penguin

Mayer, J. D., Perkins, D., Caruso, D. R., & Salovey, P. (2001). "Emotional intelligence and giftedness." *Roeper Review*, 23, 131-137.

McClelland, D. C. (1973). Testing for competence rather than intelligence. *American Psychologist*, 28(1), 1-14.

Morrison, G. S. (2001). *Early Childhood Education Today*. Upper Saddlle River, NJ: Prentice-Hall, Inc.

Murray, H. A. (1938). *Explorations in personality*. New York: Oxford University Press(2000) Naess, I. (1996, 2000). *Colour energy*. Vancouver, B.C. Canada. Colour Energy Corporation.

National Center on Secondary Education and Transition. "Part 1: What do we know about dropout prevention?" Retrieved June 20, 2007 from http://www.ncset.org/publications/essentialtools/dropout/part1.1.asp

Parker, J.D.A., Hogan, M.J., Eastabrook, J.M., Oke, A., & Wood, L.M. (2006). "Emotional intelligence and student retention: Predicting the successful transition from high school to university." *Personality and Individual Differences*, 41, 1329- 1336.

Parker, J.D.A., Creque, R.E., Barnhart, D.L., Harris, J.I., Majeski, S.A., Wood, L.M., Bond, B.J., & Hogan, M.J. (2004). "Academic achievement in high school, does emotional intelligence matter?" *Personality and Individual Differences*, 37,1321-1330.

Pert, C. (1997). *Molecules of emotion*. New York: Charles Scribner's Sons.

Peterson, C., Maier, S., & Seligman, M. (1993). *Learned helplessness*. New York: Oxford University Press.

Petrides, K. V., Frederickson, N., & Furnham, A. (2004). "The role of trait emotional intelligence in academic performance and deviant behavior at school." *Personality and Individual Differences* 36 (2004) 277-293.

Petrides, K.V., Sangareau, Y., Furnham, A., & Frederickson, N. (2006). "Trait emotional intelligence and children's peer relations at school." *Social Development*, 15 (3),537-547.

Piaget, J. (1962). *Play, dreams and imitation in childhood*. New York: Norton Press.

Power, F. C., Higgins, A., & Kohlberg, L. (1989). *Lawrence Kohlberg's Approach to Moral Education*. New York, NY: Columbia University Press

Ramey, C. T. & Ramey, S. L. (1999). *Right from birth: Building your child's foundation for life*. New York, NY: Goddard Press.

Rideout, M., (personal communication, May 30, 2002)

Rogers, C. (1980). A way of being. New York, NY: Houghton Mifflin.

Rosenthal, R. & Jacobson, L. (1966). Teachers' expectancies: Determinants of pupils' IQ gains. Psychological Reports, 19, 115-118.

Rumberger, R.W. (1987). "High school dropouts: A review of issues and evidence." *Review of Educational Research*, 57(2), 101-121.

Russ, S. W. (1998). *Affect, creative experience, and psychological adjustment*. New York, NY: Brunner/Mazel Publishers.

Russ, S. W., (1998). *Affect, creative experience, and psychological adjustment*. New York, NY: Brunner/Mazel Publishers.

Salovey, P., Bedell, B., Detweiler, J. B., & Mayer, J.D. (1999). Coping intelligently: Emotional intelligence and the coping process. In C. R. Snyder (Ed.), *Coping: The psychology of what works* (pp. 141-164). New York: Oxford University press.

Salovey, P., Mayer, J. (1990). Emotional intelligence. Imagination, cognition and personality, 9(3), 185-211. 25

Salovey, P., Mayer, J. D., Goldman, S. L., Turvey, C., & Palfai, T. p. (1995). Emotional attention, clarity, and repair: Exploring emotional intelligence using the Trait Meta-Mood Scale. In J. W. Pennebaker (Ed.), Emotion, disclosure, and health (pp.125-154). Washington, DC: American Psychological Association.

Shriver, T.P., & Weissberg, R.P. (2005, August 16). "No emotion left behind," *New York Times*,

Schulman, P. (1995). Explanatory style and achievement in school and work. In G. Buchanan & M. E. P. Seligman (Eds.), Explanatory style. Hillsdale, NJ: Lawrence Erlbaum.

Shoda, Y., Mischel, W., Peake, P. K. (1990). Predicting adolescent cognitive and Selfregulatory competencies from preschool delay of gratification: Identifying diagnostic conditions. *Developmental Psychology*, 26(6), 978-986.

Sroufe, L. A. (1997). *Emotional development: The organization of emotional life in the early years*. Cambridge, CB2 IRP: Cambridge University Press.

Steinberg, J. (1998). History of affective education. JPC, (1)1 in http://www.eqtoday.com/jpca.html.

Sternberg, R. (1996). *Successful intelligence*. New York: Simon & Schuster.

Stone, H., Parker, J.D.A., & Wood, L.M. (2005). "Report on the Ontario Principals' Council leadership study." Toronto: Ontario Principals' Council

Stone-McCown, K., Jensen, A. L., Freedman, J. M.., & Rideout, M. C. (1998). *Selfscience: The subject is me.* (2nd ed.). San Mateo, CA: 6 Seconds.

Stone, K. F., & Dillehunt, H. Q. (1978). *Self-science: The subject is me.* Santa Monica CA: Goodyear Publishing Company, Inc.

Taffel, R., & Blau, M. (1991). *Nurturing good children now.* New York: Golden Books Publishing Co., Inc.

Taylor, B. (2002). Early childhood program management. Upper Saddle River, NJ: Merrill/Prentice Hall.

Thorndike, R. L., & Stein, S. (1937). *An evaluation of the attempts to measure social intelligence.* Psychological Bulletin, 34, 275-284.

Thornton, G. C. I., & Byham, W. C. (1982). *Assessment centers and managerial performance.* New York: Academic Press.

Trice, A. D. (December, 1982). Ratings of humor following experience with unsolvable tasks. *Psychological Reports, 51*(3), Pt.2:1148.

Trinidad, D.R. & Johnson, C.A. (2002). "The association between emotional intelligence and early adolescent tobacco and alcohol use." *Personality and Individual Differences*, 32 (1), 95-105.

Tsaousis, I. & Nikolaou, I. (2005). "Exploring the relationship of emotional intelligence with physical and psychological health functioning." *Stress and Health*, March 3, Wiley InterScience.

Tunnell, M. O., Jacobs, J. S., & Darigan, D. L. (2002). Children's Literature Database: A Resource for Teachers, Parents, and Media Specialists (Second Edition) [Computer Software]. Upper Saddle River, NJ: Pearson Education, Inc.

Twerski, A. J. (2000). *Growing Each Day.* 5th Printing. Brooklyn, NY: Mesorah Publications, Ltd.

Wang, M.C., Haertel, G.D., & Walberg, H.J. (1997). Learning influences. In H.J. Walberg & G.D. Haertel (Eds.) Psychology and Educational Practice (p.199-211). Berkeley, CA: McCatchan (210).

Wechsler, D. (1940). Nonintellective factors in general intelligence. Psychological Bulletin, 37, 444-445.

Wechsler, D. (1958). The measurement and appraisal of adult intelligence. (4th Ed.). Baltimore, MD: The Williams and Wilkins Company.

Wolfe, P. (2001). *Brain matters: Translating research into classroom practice.* Alexandria, VA: Association for Supervision and Curriculum Development.

World Health Organization, Health and health behavior among young people, (monitoringthefuture.org), cited in Freedman, J. (2007). Special advice for dads in *At the Heart of Leadership: How to Get Results with Emotional Intelligence.* San Francisco: Six Seconds.

Wortham, S. C. (2002). *Early childhood curriculum: Developmental bases for learning and teaching.* (3rd Ed.). Upper Saddle River, NJ: Merrill Prentice-Hall.

FEELINGS WORDS

A

aback, abandoned, abashed, abducted, abhorred, abject, able, abnormal, abominable, about, abrasive, absent-minded, absolved, absorbed, absorbent, abstemious, abstract, abstracted, abused, abusive, abysmal, abyssal, accelerated, acceptable, accepted, accepting, accessible, accident-prone, acclaimed, acclimated, accommodated, accommodating, accomplished, accosted, accosting, accountable, accusatory, accused, accusing, acerbic, aching, acknowledged, acquiescent, acquisitive, acrimonious, activated, active, actualized, adamant, addicted, adept, adequate, admirable, admiration, admired, admiring, admonished, adorable, adored, adoring, adrift, advanced, adventurous, adverse, affable, affected, affection, affectionate, affirmed, afflicted, affluent, affronted, afraid, against, agape, aggravated, aggressive, aghast, agitated, aglow, agnostic, agog, agonized, agony, agoraphobic, agreeable, ahead, aimless, airy, alarmed, alert, alienated, alive, allied, allured, alluring, alone, aloof, altruistic, amazed, amazing, ambiguous, ambitious, ambivalent, ambushed, amenable, amiable, amorous, amused, amusing, analyzed, anarchistic, anesthetized, angry, anguish, anguished, anhedonic, animated, annihilated, annoyed, annoying, anonymous, antagonistic, antagonized, anticipation, antiquated, antisocial, antsy, anxiety, anxious, apart, apathetic, apologetic, appalled, appealed, appealing, appeased, applauded, appraised, appreciated, appreciative, apprehension, apprehensive, approachable, appropriate, approved, approved of, archaic, ardent, argued with, argumentative, aristocratic, aroused, arrogant, artful, articulate, artificial, artistic, artless, ascetic, ashamed, asinine, asocial, assaulted, assertive, assessed, assuaged, assured, astonished, astounded, at ease, at home, at peace, at peril, at risk, at war, atrophied, attached, attacked, attentive, attracted, attractive, audacious, austere, authentic, authoritarian, authoritative, autocratic, available, avaricious, avid, avoided, awake, awakened, aware, awe, awed, awesome, awestruck, awful, awkward

B

babied, backward, bad, badgered, baited, balanced, bamboozled, banished, bankrupt, banned, bantered, bare, barraged

FEELINGS WORDS

barred	bitter	brilliant	cared for	chicken
barren	blackmailed	brisk	carefree	chided
bashful	blah	bristling	careful	childish
battered	blamed	broken	careless	childlike
battle-weary	blaming	broken-down	caring	chipper
battle-worn	blank	broken-up	carried away	chivalrous
bearable	blasé,	brooding	cast	choked
beaten	blasphemous	bruised	cast out	choked-up
beaten down	blasted	brushed-off	castigated	chosen
beatific	bleak	brutal	categorized	churlish
beautiful	blind	bubbly	caught	circumspect
beckoned	bliss	bugged	cautious	circumvented
bedazzled	blissful	buggered	cavalier	civil
bedeviled	blithe	bullied	censored	civilized
befriended	blocked	bullish	censured	classy
befuddled	blown away	bullshitted	centered	claustrophobic
beguiled	blue	bummed	certain	clean
behind	boastful	bummed out	chafed	cleansed
beholden	bogus	buoyant	chagrined	clear
beleaguered	boiling	burdened	chained	clear-headed
belittled	boisterous	burdensome	challenged	clenched
belligerent	bold	buried	challenging	clever
belonging	bombastic	burned	changed	clever
beloved	bonkers	burned-out	changing	close
bemused	bored	burned-up	chaotic	closed
benevolent	boring	bursting	charged	closed in
bent	bossed-around	bushed	charismatic	closed-minded
berated	bossy	bypassed	charitable	clouded
bereaved	bothered	C	charmed	clueless
bereft	bothersome	caged	charming	clumsy
beseeched	bought	cajoled	chaste	coarse
beset	bound	calculating	chastised	cocky
besieged	bound-up	callow	chatty	coddled
besmirched	boxed-in	calm	cheap	coerced
bestial	braced	calmed down	cheapened	cold
betrayed	brainwashed	canny	cheated	cold-blooded
better	brash	cantankerous	cheated on	cold-hearted
bewildered	brave	capable	cheeky	collapsed
bewitched	brazen	capricious	cheerful	collapsing
bewitching	breathless	captious	cheerless	collected
biased	breezy	captivated	cheery	combative
big	bridled	captured	cherished	comfortable
bitchy	bright	cared about	chic	comforted

FEELINGS WORDS

comfy	conservative	coy	**D**	dehumanized
committed	considerate	cozy	daffy	dejected
common	considered	crabby	dainty	delicate
commonplace	consistent	crafty	damaged	delighted
communicative	consoled	cranky	damned	delightful
comparative	consoling	crappy	dangerous	delinquent
compared	conspicuous	crass	dared	delirious
compassionate	constrained	craving	daring	delivered
compatible	constricted	crazed	dark	deluded
compelled	constructive	crazy	dashed	demanding
competent	consumed	creative	dashing	demeaned
competitive	contained	credulous	daunted	demented
complacent	contaminated	crestfallen	dauntless	demoralized
complementary	contemplative	criminal	dazed	demoted
complete	contempt	crippled	dead	demotivated
complex	contemptible	critical	dear	demure
compliant	contemptuous	criticized	debased	denatured
complicated	content	cross	debated	denigrated
complimentary	contented	crossed	debauched	denounced
complimented	contentious	cross-examined	debilitated	denurtured
composed	contrite	crotchety	debonair	dependable
compressed	controlled	crowded	deceitful	dependent
compulsive	controlling	crucified	deceived	depleted
conceited	convenient	crude	decent	deported
concentrated	conventional	cruel	deceptive	depraved
concerned	convicted	crushed	decided	deprecated
condemned	convinced	cryptic	decimated	depreciated
condescended to	convincing	cuckoo	decrepit	depressed
condescending	cool	cuddled	dedicated	deprived
confident	cooperative	cuddly	defamed	derailed
confined	cordial	culled	defeated	derided
confirmed	cornered	culpable	defective	desecrated
confirming	correct	cultivated	defenseless	deserted
conflicted	corrupt	cultured	defensive	deserving
conforming	corrupted	cunning	deferent	desirable
confused	counterfeit	curious	defiant	desire
congenial	counter-productive	cursed	deficient	desired
connected	courageous	cut	defiled	desirous
conned	courteous	cut-down	definite	desolate
conniving	courtly	cute	deflated	despair
conquered	coveted	cut-off	deformed	despairing
conscientious	covetous	cynical	degenerate	desperate
consecrated	cowardly		degraded	despicable

FEELINGS WORDS

despised	disconnected	disobeyed	domineering	earthy
despondent	disconsolate	disorderly	done	eased
destroyed	discontent	disorganized	doomed	easy
destructive	discontented	disoriented	double-crossed	easy-going
detached	discounted	disowned	doubted	ebullient
deteriorated	discouraged	disparaged	doubtful	eccentric
determined	discredited	dispassionate	dowdy	eclectic
detest	discreet	dispensable	down	eclipsed
detestable	disdain	dispirited	downcast	ecstatic
detested	disdained	displaced	downhearted	edgy
devastated	disdainful	displeased	downtrodden	edified
deviant	disempowered	disposable	drained	edifying
devious	disenchanted	dispossessed	dramatic	educated
devoid	disenfranchised	disputed	drawn away	effaced
devoted	disentangled	disregarded	drawn back	effective
devoured	disfavored	disrespected	drawn in	effeminate
diagnosed	disgraced	disruptive	drawn toward	effervescent
dictated to	disgruntled	dissatisfied	dread	efficacious
dictatorial	disgust	dissected	dreaded	efficient
different	disgusted	dissed	dreadful	effusive
difficult	disgusting	dissident	dreamy	egocentric
diffident	disharmonious	dissociated	dreary	egotistic
dignified	disheartened	distant	dried-up	egotistical
diligent	disheveled	distorted	driven	elastic
dim	dishonest	distracted	droopy	elated
diminished	dishonorable	distraught	dropped	elderly
diplomatic	dishonored	distressed	drowning	electric
direct	disillusioned	distrusted	drubbed	electrified
directionless	disinclined	distrustful	drummed	elegant
dirty	disingenuous	disturbed	dubious	elevated
disabled	disintegritous *	diverted	dull	elitist
disaffected	disinterested	divided	dumb	eloquent
disagreeable	disjointed	divorced	dumbfounded	elusive
disappointed	dislike	docile	dumped	emancipated
disappointing	disliked	dogged	dumped on	emasculated
disapproved of	dislocated	dogmatic	duped	embarrassed
disapproving	dislodged	doleful	dutiful	embittered
disbelieved	disloyal	domestic	dwarfed	eminent
disbelieving	dismal	domesticated	dynamic	emotional
discarded	dismayed	dominant	**E**	emotionless
disciplined	dismissed	dominated	eager	emotive
discombobulated	dismissive	dominating	early	empathetic
disconcerted	disobedient	domineered	earnest	empathic

FEELINGS WORDS

emphatic	eradicated	explosive	fathered	flammable
empowered	erasable	exposed	fatherless	flappable
empty	erased	expressive	fatigued	flat
enabled	eros	expunged	fatuous	flattered
enamored	essential	extraordinary	favored	flawed
enchanted	established	extravagant	fawned	fledgling
enclosed	esteemed	extricated	fawned over	fleeced
encompassed	estranged	extroverted	fawning	flexible
encouraged	ethereal	exuberant	fear	flighty
encroached upon	euphoric	exultant	feared	flippant
encumbered	evaded	**F**	fearful	flipped-out
endangered	evaluated	fabulous	fearless	flirtatious
energetic	evasive	facetious	fed up	floored
energized	evicted	factious	feeble	floundering
enervated	evil	failful *	feeling	flourishing
engaged	eviscerated	faint	feisty	flush
engrossed	exacerbated	fainthearted	felicitous	flustered
enhanced	exacerbating	fair	feminine	fluttering
enigmatic	examined	faithful	fermenting	focused
enjoyment	exasperated	fake	ferocious	focussed
enlightened	exasperating	fallen	fervent	foiled
enmeshed	excellent	fallible	festive	followed
ennobled	excessive	fallow	fettered	fond
enraged	excitable	False	fickle	foolhardy
enraptured	excited	falsely	fidgety	foolish
enriched	excluded	falsely	fiendish	forbidden
enslaved	excoriated	falsely accused	fierce	forced
entangled	exculpated	faltering	fiery	forceful
enterprising	execrated	famished	filthy	foreign
entertained	exempt	famous	fine	fore-sighted
enthralled	exempted	fanatical	finicky	forgetful
enthusiastic	exhausted	fanciful	finished	forgettable
enticed	exhilarated	fantabulous	fired	forgivable
entitled	exiled	fantasizing	firm	forgiven
entombed	exonerated	fantastic	first	forgiving
entrapped	exorcised	farcical	first-class	forgotten
entrenched	exotic	fascinated	first-rate	forlorn
entrepreneurial	expansive	fascinating	fit	formed
entrusted	expectant	fascination	fixated	formidable
envied	experienced	fashionable	flabbergasted	forsaken
envious	experimental	fast	flagellated	
equipped	exploitative	fastidious	flaky	
equitable	exploited	fatalistic	flamboyant	

FEELINGS WORDS

forgotten	fussy	greedy	hard-working	hindered
forlorn	futile	gregarious	hardy	hoaxed
formed	**G**	grief	harmless	hollow
formidable	gallant	grief-stricken	harmonious	homely
forsaken	galled	grieved	harnessed	homesick
fortified	game	grieving	harried	honest
fortunate	gauche	grim	hassled	honorable
forward	gaudy	groovy	hasty	honored
fouled-up	gawky	gross	hate	hoodwinked
fractured	gay	grossed-out	hated	hopeful
fragile	generous	grotesque	hateful	hopeless
fragmented	genial	grouchy	hatred	horrible
frail	gentle	grounded	haughty	horrified
framed	genuine	groveling	haunted	horror
frank	giddy	grumpy	headstrong	horror-stricken
frantic	gifted	guarded	heady	hospitable
fraudulent	giggly	guided	healed	hostile
frazzled	gilded	guilt-free	health-conscious	hot-headed
free	giving	guiltless	healthy	hounded
frenetic	glad	guilt-tripped	heard	huge
frenzied	glamorous	guilty	heartbroken	humane
fresh	gleeful	gullible	heartened	humble
fretful	glib	gushy	heartful	humbled
fretting	gloomy	gutless	heartless	humiliated
friendless	glorious	gutsy	heartsick	humored
friendly	glowing	gutted	heart-to-heart	humorous
frightened	glum	gypped	hearty	hung up
frigid	gluttonous	**H**	heavy	hungry
frisky	goaded	haggard	heavy-hearted	hunted
frivolous	good	haggled	heckled	hurried
frolicsome	good-looking	hallowed	heeded	hurt
frowning	good-natured	hampered	held dear	hustled
frugal	gorgeous	handicapped	helped	hyped-up
frustrated	graceful	hapless	helpful	hyper
fulfilled	gracious	happy	helpless	hyperactive
full	graded	happy-go-lucky	henpecked	hypervigilent
fuming	grand	harangued	herded	hypnotized
fun	grandiose	harassed	heroic	hypocritical
funky	granted	hard	hesitant	hysterical
funloving	grateful	hardened	hideous	
funny	gratified	hard-headed	high	
furious	grave	hard-hearted	high-spirited	
fury	great	hard-pressed	hilarious	

FEELINGS WORDS

I

idealistic
idiosyncratic
idiotic
idolized
ignorant
ignored
ill
ill at ease
ill-humored
illicit
ill-tempered
imaginative
imbalanced
immaculate
immature
immobile
immobilized
immodest
immoral
immortal
immune
impaired
impartial
impassioned
impassive
impatient
impeccable
impeded
impelled
imperfect
imperiled
imperious
impermanent
impermeable
impertinent
imperturbable
impervious
impetuous
impious
implacable
impolite
important
imposed-upon
imposing
impotent
impressed
imprisoned
impudent
impugned
impulsive
impure
in
in a huff
in a quandary
in a stew
in control
in despair
in doubt
in fear
in harmony
in pain
in the dumps
in the way
in touch
in tune
inaccessible
inadequate
inappropriate
inattentive
incapable
incapacitated
incensed
incoherent
incommunicative
incompetent
incomplete
inconclusive
inconsiderate
inconsistent
inconsolable
inconspicuous
inconvenienced
inconvenient
incorrect
incorrigible
incredible
incredulous
inculcated
indebted
indecent
indecisive
indefinite
independent
indescribable
indestructible
indicted
indifferent
indignant
indirect
indiscreet
indoctrinated
indolent
indulgent
industrious
inebriated
ineffective
inept
infallible
infamous
infantile
infantilized
infatuated
infected
inferior
infirm
inflamed
inflammatory
inflated
inflexible
influenced
influential
informed
infuriated
infused
ingenious
ingenuous
inhibited
inhospitable
inhumane
inimical
injured
innocent
innovative
inquiring
inquisitive
insane
insatiable
insecure
insensitive
inside-out
insightful
insignificant
insincere
insistent
insolent
insouciant
inspired
instilled
instructive
insufficient
insulted
insulting
insurgent
intact
integritous *
intellectual
intelligent
intense
intent
interested
interesting
interfered with
interfering
interrelated
interrogated
interrupted
intimate
intimidated
intimidating
intolerant
intrepid
intrigued
introspective
introverted
intruded upon
intrusive
intuitive
invalidated
invalidating
inventive
invigorated
invisible
invited
inviting
involved
invulnerable
irascible
irate
irked
irrational
irreligious
irreproachable
irresistible
irresolute
irresponsible
irreverent
irritable
irritated
isolated

J

jaded
jaundiced
jaunty
jealous
jealousy
jeered
jeopardized
jerked around
jilted
jinxed
jittery
jocular
jolly
jolted
jostled

FEELINGS WORDS

jovial	late	loose	manic	mischievous
joyful	laughed at	loosed	manipulable	misdiagnosed
joyless	lavished	lorded over	manipulated	miserable
joyous	lax	lost	manipulative	miserly
jubilant	lazy	loud	manly	misgiving
judged	leaned on	lousy	marauding	misinformed
judgmental	leaning	lovable	marauding	misinterpreted
judicious	lecherous	loved	marginalized	misled
juggled	lectured to	loveless	married	misrepresented
jumpy	leery	lovely	marvelous	mistaken
just	left out	loving	masochistic	mistreated
justified	legitimate	low	masterful	mistrusted
K	let down	lowly	materialistic	mistrustful
keen	lethargic	low-spirited	maternal	misunderstood
kept	level-headed	loyal	mature	misused
kept away	lewd	luckless	maudlin	mixed-up
kept out	liable	lucky	meager	mobilized
kicked	liberal	ludicrous	mean	mocked
kicked around	liberated	luminous	mechanical	mocking
kidded	licentious	lured	medicated	modern
kind	lied about	luring	mediocre	modest
kindhearted	lied to	lust	meditative	molded
kindly	lifeless	lustful	meek	molested
kinky	lifted	lusty	melancholic	mollified
knackered	light	lynched	melancholy	monitored
knocked	light-hearted	**M**	melded	monopolized
knocked down	likable	macho	mellow	moody
knocked out	liked	mad	melodramatic	moping
knowledgeable	limited	made fun of	menaced	moral
L	limp	magical	menacing	moralistic
labeled	lionhearted	magnificent	merciful	**N**
lackadaisical	listened to	maimed	merry	nagged
lacking	listless	maladjusted	mesmerized	nailed
lackluster	lively	malcontent	messy	naive
lagging behind	livid	malevolent	methodical	naked
laid-back	loath	malicious	meticulous	nameless
lambasted	loathed	malignant	micro-managed	nannied
lame	loathsome	maligned	miffed	narcissistic
lamentful *	logical	manageable	mighty	narrow-minded
lamenting	lonely	managed	mindful	nasty
languid	lonesome	managerial	minimized	natural
languishing	longing	mangled	mirthful	naughty
lascivious	loopy	maniacal	misanthropic	nauseated

FEELINGS WORDS

neat	obeyed	orphaned	**P**	
needed	objectified *	ostentatious	pacified	permanent
needled	obligated	ostracized	paid off	permeable
needy	obliged	ousted	pain	perplexed
negated	obliging	out of balance	pained	persecuted
negative	obliterated	out of control	paired	persevering
neglected	oblivious	out of place	paired-off	persistent
negligent	obnoxious	out of sorts	paired-up	persnickety
nervous	obscene	out of touch	pampered	perspicuous
nervy	obscured	out of tune	panic	persuaded
nestled	observant	outdone	panicked	persuasive
nettled	observed	outgoing	panicky	pert
neurotic	obsessed	outlandish	paralyzed	perturbed
neutral	obsessive	outnumbered	paranoid	perverted
nice	obstinate	outraged	pardoned	pervious
niggardly	obstructed	outrageous	parsimonious	pessimistic
nihilistic	obvious	outranked	partial	pestered
nit-picked	odd	outspoken	passed-over	petrified
nit-picking	off	over	passionate	petty
nit-picky	off the hook	overanxious	passive	petulant
noble	offended	overbearing	pastoral	philanthropic
noisy	offensive	overcome	paternal	phlegmatic
nomadic	officious	over-controlled	pathetic	phony
nonchalant	okay	over-done	patient	picked apart
noncommittal	old	overdrawn	patronized	picked on
nonconforming	old-fashioned	overestimated	peaceful	pierced
nonplused	omnipotent	overjoyed	pedantic	pigeon-holed
normal	on	overloaded	pedestalized *	pillaged
nosey	on call	overlooked	pedestrian	pillaging
nosey	on display	overpowered	peeved	pious
nostalgic	on time	over-protected	peevish	pissed off
nothing	one-upped	over-ruled	pell-mell	piteous
noticed	open	oversensitive	penetrable	pitied
nourished	open-minded	over-simplified	penetrated	pitiful
nourishing	opinionated	overwhelmed	pensive	pitiless
numb	opportunistic	overworked	perceived	pity
numbed	opposed	overwrought	perceptive	placated
nursed	oppressed	owed	peremptory	placid
nurturing	optimistic	owing	perfect	plagued
nuts	opulent	owned	perfectionistic	plain
nutty	orderly	owning	perilous	planless
O	organized	owning	peripheral	playful
obedient	ornery		perky	pleading

FEELINGS WORDS

pleasant	primitive	pulled	questioning	realistic
pleased	prissy	pulled ahead	quick	reasonable
pliable	pristine	pulled apart	quiescent	reassured
pliant	private	pulled away	quiet	rebellious
plumbed	privileged	pulled back	quietened	reborn
plundered	privy	pulled down	quirky	rebounding
plundering	prized	pulled forward	quivery	rebuffed
plunging	proactive	pulled in	quixotic	rebuked
plush	probationary	pulverized	quizzed	recalcitrant
poised	probationed	pumped	quizzical	receptive
poisoned	probed	pumped up	**R**	reckless
polite	productive	punctual	rad	reclusive
pompous	profane	punished	radiant	recognized
pontifical	professional	pure	radical	reconciled
poor	progressing	purged	rage	recruited
popular	progressive	purposeful	raging	redeemed
porous	progress-minded	pursuant	raided	red-hot
positive	promiscuous	pursued	railroaded	reduced
possessed	promised	pushed	raked	re-enforced
possessionless	promoted	pushed ahead	raked-over	refined
possessive	promotional	pushed away	rambunctious	reflective
potent	prone to	pushed back	rancid	refreshed
pouty	propagandistic	pushed forward	ransacked	regimented
powerful	propagandized	pushed in	rapacious	regressing
powerless	propelled	pushy	raped	regressive
practical	proper	put away	rapt	regret
praised	prosaic	put down	rapture	regretful
preached to	prosecuted	put down	rapturous	rejectable
precarious	prosperous	put out	rare	rejected
precious	prostituted	put upon	rash	rejecting
precluded	protected	puzzled	rated	rejoiced
precocious	protective	**Q**	rational	rejoicing
preoccupied	proud	quaking	rattled	rejuvenated
prepared	provincial	qualified	raunchy	relaxed
pressed	provisional	quandary	ravenous	released
pressured	provocative	quarantined	ravished	reliable
presumptuous	provoked	quarrelsome	ravishing	reliant
pretentious	prudish	quashed	raw	relieved
pretty	psyched	queasy	reachable	religious
preyed upon	psychopathic	queer	reactionary	reluctant
prim	psychotic	queried	reactive	remedied
primal	puerile	querulous	ready	reminiscent
primary	puffed up	questioned	real	remiss

FEELINGS WORDS

remorse	retarded	sacrificed	secure	sensuous
remorseful	reticent	sacrificial	seduced	sentenced
remorseless	retired	sacrilegious	seductive	sentimental
remote	reunited	sad	seething	separated
removed	revengeful	sadistic	seized	serene
renewed	revered	safe	selected	serious
repelled	reverent	sanctimonious	selective	servile
repentant	reviled	sane	self-absorbed	set
replaceable	revitalized	sanguine	self-acceptance	set up
replaced	revived	sarcastic	self-acceptant	settled
replenished	revolted	sardonic	self-assured	sexy
reprehensible	revolting	sassy	self-centered	shadowed
repressed	revolutionary	sated	self-confident	shaken
reprimanded	rewarded	satiated	self-conscious	shaky
reproached	rich	satisfied	self-deprecating	shallow
reproved	ridden	saucy	self-depreciating	shamed
repugnant	ridiculed	saved	self-destructive	shameful
repulsed	ridiculous	savvy	self-disciplined	shaped
repulsive	right	scandalized	self-effacing	sharp
rescued	righteous	scapegoated	self-expressed	shattered
resented	rigid	scared	self-flagellating	sheepish
resentful	rigorous	scarred	self-forgiving	sheltered
reserved	riled	scattered	self-hate	shielded
resigned	rivested	scheming	self-hating	shocked
resilient	riveted	scolded	self-hatred	shook-up
resistant	robbed	scorn	self-important	shot-down
resisting	robust	scorned	self-indulgent	shouted at
resolute	romantic	scornful	selfish	shrewd
resolved	rotten	screwed	selfless	shunned
resourceful	rough	screwed over	self-loathing	shut out
respected	rowdy	screwed up	self-love	shy
respectful	rubricized	scrutinized	self-pitying	sick
responsible	rude	sealed in	self-pleasing	sickened
responsive	rueful	sealed off	self-rejection	significant
rested	ruined	sealed out	self-reliant	silenced
restful	ruled	sealed out	self-righteous	silent
restive	run down	sealed up	self-sacrificing	silly
restless	run out	seared	self-serving	simple
restrained	run over	second	self-understandin	simplified
restricted	rushed	secondary	senile	sincere
retaliated	ruthless	second-class	sensible	sinful
retaliated against	S	second-guessed	sensitive	single
retaliatory	sabotaged	second-rate	sensual	singled-out

FEELINGS WORDS

sinking	soothed	sterile	subdued	sympathy
skeptical	sophisticated	stern	subjugated	**T**
skilled	sophomoric	stewing	submissive	tempestuous
skillful	sophomoric	stiff	subordinate	tender
slack	sore	stifled	subordinated	tense
slain	sorrow	stigmatized	subservient	terse
slandered	sorrowful	still	subtle	testy
slaughtered	sorry	stilted	subversive	thankful
sleazy	sough	stimulated	successful	thick
slighted	sound	stingy	suffering	third-class
sloppy	sour	stodgy	suffocated	thorough
slothful	soured	stoic	suicidal	thoughtful
slovenly	spared	stomped on	sulky	threadbare
slow	sparkling	stonewalled	sullen	threatened
sluggish	spartan	stout	sullied	thrilled
small	spastic	stout hearted	sunk	thunderous
smart	special	straight-laced	sunny	ticklish
smart-alecky	speechless	strained	super	tidy
smashed	spellbound	stranded	superb	time-worn
smitten	spent	strange	supercilious	tingly
smooth	spineless	strangled	superficial	tipsy
smothered	spirited	strengthened	superior	tired
smug	spiritless	stressed	superseded	tireless
snapped at	spiteful	stretched	superstitious	titillated
sneaky	splendid	stricken	supported	tolerable
snobbish	spoiled	strict	supportive	topsy-turvey
snobby	spontaneous	stroked	suppressed	torrential
snoopy	spooked	strong	sure	tragic
snowed	spunky	strong-armed	surly	trampled
snubbed	squashed	strong-willed	surpassed	tranquil
snuggled	squeamish	stubborn	surprised	transitory
soaring	squeezed	stuck	surrendered	trapped
sociable	squelched	stuck-up	surveyed	traumatic
social	stable	studious	susceptible	tricked
sodden	stained	stuffed	suspicious	trivial
soft	stale	stumped	sulky	true
soft-hearted	stalked	stunned	sultry	truthful
sold	startled	stunning	swallowed up	turbocharged
sold-out	starved	stunted	sweet	twisted
solemn	steamed-up	stupefied	swell	tyranical
solid	stepped-on	stupid	switched on	
solitary	stepped-over	stylish	sycophantic	
somber	stereotyped	suave	sympathetic	

FEELINGS WORDS

U

ubiquitous	unhappy		
unabashed	unharmonious		
Unable	unhasty		
Unacquainted	unhealthy		
Unadorned	unholy		
Unafraid	unimpaired		
Unaided	unknowing		
unambiguous	unleashed		
unashamed	unlucky		
unbound	unmatched		
unbreakable	unobstructed		
unclean	unorthodox		
uncomfortable	unparagoned		
uncomely	unprincipled		
uncompassionate	unproductive		
unconcerned	unprogressive		
unconsidered	unprotected		
uncultured	unqualified		
undaunted	unrestful		
undermined	unrighteous		
undersexed	unruffled		
understanding	unruly		
understood	unsafe		
undervalued	unsatiated		
undeveloped	unstable		
undisguised	unsteady		
undomesticated	unsure		
uneasy	unswayable		
unennobled	unsympathetic		
unfaithful	untidy		
unfaltering	untiring		
unfamed	untouched		
unfamiliar	unusual		
unfeeling	unwholesome		
unfertile	unwilling		
unfit	unwise		
unflappable	upbeat		
unfortunate	uplifted		
unfounded	upright		
unfruitful	upset		
ungrateful	upside-down		
ungratified	uptight		
unhallowed	useful		
unhampered	utopian		

V

vacant	weighed-down
vacillating	weightless
vacuous	weird
vain	whetted
valid	whipped
valorous	whole
valuable	whole-souled
valueless	wicked
vanquished	wieldy
vehement	wiggley
venerable	wild
veracious	willing
verbose	wily
versatile	winsome
vertiginous	wise
vexed	wishy-washy
vicious	wistful
victimized	witching
vigorous	witchy
villaious	withdrawn
vindictive	witty
violated	woeful
virtuous	wondrous
virulent	worldly
visionary	worldly-wise
vital	worried
vitiated	worthless
vivacious	worthy
vociferous	wreakful
void	wrecked
voracious	wretched
vulgar	wronged
vulturous	wry

W

waggish

X

xenophobic

waned

Y

wanting	yanked
warlike	yeasty
warm	yernful
wary	youthful
wasted	yummy
watchful	

Z

weak	zany
weary	zealous
	zippy
	zoetic
	zonked

$28.00
ISBN 978-0-578-07644-7

www.ingramcontent.com/pod-product-compliance
Lightning Source LLC
Chambersburg PA
CBHW041533220426
43662CB00002B/44